Be A Better Reader

Level C

Seventh Edition

Nila Banton Smith

Globe Fearon Educational Publishers
A Division of Simon & Schuster
Upper Saddle River, New Jersey

Pronunciation Key

Symbol	Key Word	Respelling
a	act	(akt)
ah	star	(stahr)
ai	dare	(dair)
aw	also	(awl soh)
ay	flavor	(flay vər)
e	end	(end)
ee	eat	(eet)
er	learn	(lern)
	sir	(ser)
	fur	(fer)
i	hit	(hit)
eye	idea	(eye dee ə)
y	like	(lyk)
ir	deer	(dir)
	fear	(fir)
oh	open	(oh pen)
oi	foil	(foil)
	boy	(boi)
or	horn	(horn)
ou	out	(out)
	flower	(flou ər)
oo	hoot	(hoot)
	rule	(rool)
yoo	few	(fyoo)
	use	(yooz)

Symbol	Key Word	Respelling
u	book	(buk)
	put	(put)
uh	cup	(kuhp)
ə	a as in along	(ə lawng)
	e as in moment	(moh mənt)
	i as in modify	(mahd ə fy)
	o as in protect	(prə tekt)
	u as in circus	(ser kəs)
ch	chill	(chil)
g	go	(goh)
j	joke	(johk)
	bridge	(brij)
k	kite	(kyt)
	cart	(kahrt)
ng	bring	(bring)
s	sum	(suhm)
	cent	(sent)
sh	sharp	(shahrp)
th	thin	(thin)
z	zebra	(zee brə)
	pose	(pohz)
zh	treasure	(treszh ər)

Be A Better Reader, Level C, Seventh Edition
Nila Banton Smith

Printed in the United States of America

9 10   99 00 01

C12
ISBN 0-8359-1922-6

Acknowledgments

We wish to express our appreciation for permission to use and adapt copyrighted materials.

The dictionary definitions in this book are reprinted with permission of Macmillan Reference USA, a Division of Simon & Schuster, from WEBSTER'S NEW WORLD DICTIONARY, Basic School Edition. Copyright © 1983 by Simon & Schuster Inc.

A & W Publishers for the almanac entry. Reprinted by permission of A & W Publishers, Inc., from INFORMATION PLEASE ALMANAC 1982. Copyright © 1981 by Simon & Schuster, a Viacom Company.

Photo Credits

p. 12: UPI/Bettmann, p. 13: (*left*) NASA/The Image Works, (*right*) AP/Wide World; p. 18: Neg. No. 126941, Courtesy of American Museum of Natural History (Photo: AMNH–Sinclair Aerial Survey); p. 28: UPI/Bettmann; p. 40: Archive Photos; p. 42: AP/Wide World; p. 68: The Granger Collection; p. 73: Alexander Farnsworth/The Image Works; p. 74: Margot Granitsas/Photo Researchers Inc.; p. 97: UPI/Bettmann; p. 98: The Bettmann Archive; p. 133: David Madison/DUOMO; p. 139: Ken Karp; p. 159: (*left*) Ken Karp, (*right*) IBM Archives; p. 160: IBM Archives; p. 161: (*top*) UPI/Bettmann, (*bottom left*) Don Smetzer/Tony Stone Images, (*bottom right*) Superstock.

Contents

3

How to Use *Be A Better Reader*

For more than thirty years, *Be A Better Reader* has helped students improve their reading skills. *Be A Better Reader* teaches the comprehension and study skills that you need to read and enjoy all types of materials—from library books to the different textbooks that you will encounter in school.

To get the most from *Be A Better Reader*, you should know how the lessons are organized. As you read the following explanations, it will be helpful to look at some of the lessons.

In each of the first four lessons of a unit, you will apply an important skill to a reading selection in literature, social studies, science, or mathematics. Each of these lessons includes the following seven sections.

Skill Focus

This section teaches you a specific skill. You should read the Skill Focus carefully, paying special attention to words that are printed in boldface type. The Skill Focus tells you about a skill that you will use when you read the selection.

Word Clues

This section teaches you how to recognize and use different types of context clues. These clues will help you with the meanings of the underlined words in the selection.

Reading a Literature, Social Studies, Science, or Mathematics Selection

This section introduces the selection that you will read and gives you suggestions about what to look for as you read. The suggestions will help you understand the selection.

Selection

The selections in the literature lessons are similar to those in a literature anthology, library book, newspaper, or magazine. The social studies selec-tions are like chapters in a social studies textbook or encyclopedia. They often include maps and tables. The science selections, like a science textbook, include special words in boldface type and sometimes diagrams. The mathematics selections will help you acquire skill in reading mathematics textbooks.

Recalling Facts

Answers to the questions in this section—the first of three activity sections—can be found in the selection. You will sometimes have to reread parts of the selection to do this activity.

Interpreting Facts

The second activity includes questions whose answers are not directly stated in the selection. For these questions, you must combine the information in the selection with what you already know in order to *infer* the answers.

Skill Focus Activity

In the last activity, you will use the skill that you learned in the Skill Focus section at the beginning of the lesson to answer questions about the selection. If you have difficulty completing this activity, reread the Skill Focus section.

The remaining lessons in each unit give you practice with such skills as using a dictionary, an encyclopedia, and other reference materials; using phonics and syllabication aids in recognizing new words; locating and organizing information; and adjusting reading rate. Other reading skills that are necessary in everyday experience are also covered, such as reading a bus schedule and a menu.

Each time that you learn a new skill in *Be A Better Reader*, look for opportunities to use the skill in your other reading at school and at home. Your reading ability will improve the more you practice reading!

Lesson 1

Plot

Reading a Literature Selection

▶ **Background Information**

A myth is a story created to dramatize the central conflicts of human life. Myths are handed down through the centuries. The story that you will read is a Greek myth that is over five thousand years old.

▶ **Skill Focus**

The plan of action or series of events in a story is called the **plot**. In most stories, the plot follows a basic pattern.

1. **Beginning:** The beginning introduces the main character and the conflict and establishes the setting.
2. **Rising Action:** The plot begins to build as the conflict develops. The main character struggles to achieve a goal or to solve a problem.
3. **Climax:** The climax marks the story's turning point. After the climax, you are often able to predict how the story will end.
4. **Falling Action:** The events after the climax focus on how the main character resolves the story's conflict.

5. **Conclusion:** A final event ties together all loose ends. If you drew the plot of a story, it would look like this.

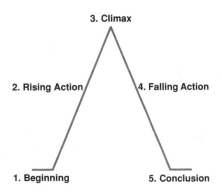

3. Climax
2. Rising Action
4. Falling Action
1. Beginning
5. Conclusion

Use the diagram above and the following questions to help you follow the plot of a story.

1. What do you know about the story's setting and characters at the beginning?
2. What conflict develops as the story's action rises?
3. What is the climax?
4. How is the conflict resolved as the action falls?
5. Is the story's conclusion appropriate?

▶ **Word Clues**

When you read, you may come across a word that names a special person, place, or thing. If the paragraph has no context clues to explain the word, there may be a clue elsewhere. Read the sentence below.

> With a fist of iron, he ruled the kingdom of Crete.[1]

Notice that there is a raised number after the word *Crete*. This is a signal to look at the bottom of the page for a footnote with the same number. A footnote gives a brief definition or explanation.

[1] Crete (KREET) an island southeast of Greece.

Use **footnote** context clues to find the meaning of the three other numbered words in the selection.

▶ **Strategy Tip**

As you read, "The Flight of Daedalus," use the diagram and the five questions in the Skill Focus to help you follow the plot. When you think the story has reached its climax, try to predict the conclusion. Doing this exercise will help you understand the story better.

The Flight of Daedalus

Long, long ago lived a proud and terrible king. His name was Minos. With a fist of iron, he ruled the kingdom of Crete.[1]

Daedalus, another proud man, also lived on the island of Crete. He was a sculptor and a builder. He may have been the finest builder of his time. Daedalus built many fine buildings for King Minos.

The most famous structure that Daedalus built for Minos was the Labyrinth.[2] It was designed as a prison and a trap. No one could find a way out of its passageways without knowing the design. Minos imprisoned his enemies there.

One day Minos became very angry with Daedalus. The builder had given away the secret of the Labyrinth. In anger, Minos imprisoned Daedalus in the Labyrinth. Within a short time, however, Daedalus managed to escape. Minos had been foolish to imagine that Daedalus could not escape from his own trap.

The sculptor found his son, Icarus, and planned to flee from Crete. But Minos was determined to recapture Daedalus. The king's soldiers searched all the ships before they left the island.

Minos knew that Daedalus and Icarus were hiding in the countryside, but he didn't care. He was sure that Daedalus and Icarus could not escape from Crete. So Minos decided to let Daedalus wander free for a while. "Soon the master builder will realize that he is trapped here. He will have to admit that he is in my power and will give himself up. Then I will give him many difficult tasks to perform."

Daedalus tried many times to find a way to escape from the island. He stood on the rocky hills of Crete and stared out to sea. Above him, the sea gulls and other sea birds wheeled and dipped in the sky. Below, the sun glistened on the water in the harbor and on the helmets of Minos' soldiers. Daedalus could see the trap that Minos had set.

1 Crete (KREET): an island southeast of Greece.
2 Labyrinth (LAB ə rinth): a building on ancient Crete with many winding passages and blind alleys; a maze.

"I cannot let Minos get the better of me," he thought. "I must escape with my son. There must be a way off the island."

At times, Daedalus feared that he and his son would be captives on Crete forever. But his quick mind kept searching for a way out. As he pondered, he watched the many birds that soared high in the blue sky. Suddenly, Daedalus was struck by a thought. "Minos may rule the land and sea, but he cannot control the air!" Daedalus said, as he watched feathers drop from the wings of the sea gulls.

He quickly sent his son Icarus in search of stray sea-gull feathers. Icarus found tiny, soft feathers. He picked up long, strong feathers. He gathered black plumes and white ones. He found blue feathers and brown feathers. Soon, Icarus had made a great mound of feathers of all kinds.

Then Daedalus set to work. He built a large wooden frame shaped like a bird's wing. He fastened feathers to it. Some he sewed on; others he stuck on with wax. Finally, he used wax to mold all the feathers into shape. Once he had finished this frame, he made another one and covered it with feathers, too. Now, he had two huge wings, like those of a giant bird.

Daedalus fastened the wings to his shoulders. Would they work? He flapped the wings and tried to fly. After some minutes, the wings lifted him from the ground.

He could fly! But Daedalus soon learned that there was more to flying than flapping his wings. He had to learn to swoop, to soar on the winds, to turn and gather speed.

With all haste, Daedalus made wings for Icarus. Icarus watched gleefully as his father sewed and glued the feathers in place. Icarus could scarcely wait to put on the wonderful wings.

At last, the wings were finished. Daedalus fastened them to his son's shoulders. Icarus looked very handsome. The beautiful wings covered his entire body. His golden hair shone in the sunlight, and his eyes sparkled with excitement.

Icarus learned to fly in no time. He seemed to have been born to it. His father, knowing how daring Icarus could be, warned him often to be careful. "Don't fly too close to the water," he would say. "The fog will weigh you down. And don't fly close to the sun. Its warmth will melt the wax on your wings."

Icarus listened impatiently to his father's warnings. He thought, "I can take care of myself!"

One fair morning, Daedalus said, "The wind is just right today. We shall fly to Sicily."[3]

Strapping on their wings, Daedalus and Icarus walked to the top of a rocky hill. Daedalus flapped his huge wings, rose in the air, and flew out over the sea. Icarus lifted himself with his wings and followed. Minos could never catch them now!

Daedalus headed out over the ocean, beating the air strongly and surely. Icarus swooped and turned as he followed his father. Flying free in the air, Icarus knew the joy of being a bird. He looked down at the white-capped waves. How wonderful to be soaring above them! Then he looked at the clouds above. How exciting it would be to fly above them!

> Flying free in the air, Icarus knew the joy of being a bird.

Icarus forgot his father's warnings. Beating his wings faster and faster, he rose up and up. As he flew higher, the sun flickered and gleamed on his feathers. On and on he flew, higher and higher. The sun grew brighter.

The air became very warm, but Icarus flew on. As he flew, it became more and more difficult to climb higher. His wings drooped. Feathers began to fall like snowflakes. The sun's heat was melting the wax! Furiously, Icarus beat his wings, but they could no longer support him. As he fell toward the glittering ocean far below, Icarus cried out to his father.

Daedalus heard the cry and turned. He caught only a glimpse of his son as Icarus plunged into the white-capped waves. Nothing

[3] Sicily (SIS əl ee): an island south of Italy.

remained except a few feathers floating on the surface.

In deep grief, Daedalus flew on to Sicily. He went to the temple of the sun god Apollo.[4]

[4] Apollo (ə POL oh): a Greek god; the son of Zeus, king of the gods.

There he hung up his wings as an offering to the god.

Daedalus had beaten his enemy, Minos, but at the terrible cost of the life of his son. Perhaps the gods were punishing Daedalus for daring to do something mere mortals were not meant to do: fly with the wings of a bird.

RECALLING FACTS

Write the answers to the following questions on the lines provided. You may go back to the selection to find an answer.

1. Identify the three story characters.

_____, King of Crete

_____, a master builder

_____, his son

2. What did the builder make for the king that pleased the king very much?

_____

3. Why was Daedalus imprisoned?

_____

_____

4. How did Daedalus attach feathers to the wings?

_____

_____

_____

5. What caused the feathers to drop from Icarus' wings?

_____

_____

_____

_____

_____

6. Complete each statement with the correct word.

Apollo   Sicily   Labyrinth

a. Archaeologists think they have discovered the original

_____ on a mountainside in Crete.

b. In Greek mythology, _____ is the god of light and the sun.

c. The Strait of Messina separates

_____ from the mainland of Italy.

INTERPRETING FACTS

Not all the questions about a story are answered directly in the story. For the following questions, you will have to figure out answers not stated directly in the story. Write questions on the lines provided.

1. Below are two proverbs. Circle the one that fits the story. Explain your answer.
   a. Haste makes waste.
   b. Pride goes before a fall.

_____

_____

2. For all the three characters in the story, state how pride caused their downfall, or defeat.

_____

_____

3. Why did Icarus ignore his father's warnings?

_____

4. Why didn't Daedalus, like Icarus, forget himself and fly too close to the sun?

_____

5. Do you think that Daedalus ever flew again? Explain your answer. Use an event from the story to support your answer.

_____

_____

SKILL FOCUS

Below are some of the events in the myth of Daedalus. Write the letter of the appropriate event on the lines provided in the plot diagram. It may help if you first decide which event is the climax.

    a. Daedalus escapes from the Labyrinth.

    b. Daedalus sees Icarus fall into the sea.

    c. Daedalus builds two pairs of wings to help him and Icarus escape from Crete.

    d. Daedalus hangs up his wings as an offering to the sun god Apollo.

    e. With their wings, Daedalus and Icarus head for Sicily.

    f. Icarus, ignoring Daedalus' warnings, flies too close to the sun.

    g. Alone, Daedalus flies to Sicily.

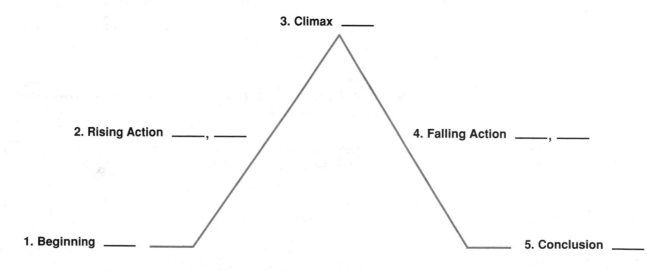

3. Climax _____

2. Rising Action _____, _____

4. Falling Action _____, _____

1. Beginning _____

5. Conclusion _____

▶ **Real Life Connections** Describe one way in which pride hurt someone you know.

Comparing and Contrasting

Reading a Social Studies Selection

▶ Background Information

The history of flight was made by brave and daring individuals. The selection that you are about to read discusses Amelia Earhart and Sally Ride, both pioneers of flying. In 1932, Amelia Earhart became the first woman to fly solo across the Atlantic Ocean. During her life, Earhart set many other flight records as well. As an astronaut, Sally Ride made history in our time. She was the first American woman to fly in space. She now teaches physics. As you read "Flying to Fame," draw comparisons and contrasts between the two women.

▶ Skill Focus

To **compare** is to find what is alike between two or more things. To **contrast** is to find what is different between two or more things. Comparing and contrasting is something that you do every day.

When you wake up, you look outside or turn on the television to find out if the weather is either the same as or different from yesterday's weather. When you shop, you compare and contrast items: are these two sweaters that cost the same really the same, or is one of them better?

When reading a social studies selection, you will often need to compare or contrast two or more people, places, or events. Remember that when you compare, you look for what is similar. When you contrast, you look for differences.

A writer sometimes presents material about two topics separately. The writer may discuss two people one at a time, each in a separate paragraph. The writer might describe the childhood, education, and achievements of one person first. Then the writer would give the same information for the other person.

When you read material organized in this way, keep in mind the similarities and differences between the two people being discussed. Because information about each person is given in a separate section, you must draw the comparisons and contrasts.

▶ Word Clues

When you read a word that you do not know, look for context clues to help you understand it.

Context clues are words near the unknown word that make its meaning clearer. Read the sentence below.

> Sally Ride <u>donned</u> her space suit and her bubble helmet with the ease that you slip on a coat and hat.

If you do not know the meaning of the word *donned*, the phrase *with the ease that you slip on a coat and hat* can help you. You can figure out the meaning of *donned* from the details in the phrase that follows it. You can tell that *donned* means "to put on."

Use **detail** context clues to find the meaning of the three underlined words in the selection.

▶ Strategy Tip

When reading textbooks, you may find words that are difficult to say. These words are usually respelled to help you pronounce them. The pronunciation key on page 2 will help you learn how to pronounce these difficult words.

FLYING TO FAME

Amelia Earhart and Sally Ride, pioneers of flight, have pushed back the boundaries of the world and the universe. These two women are also pioneers for their gender. They have proven that women, as well as men, have the courage and determination to make history.

✗ In 1932, a young woman named Amelia Earhart set off on a dangerous flight. She pulled on her leather flying gear, adjusted her goggles, and climbed into her propeller plane. Alone, she took off from Newfoundland, Canada, to cross the Atlantic Ocean. The world cheered when Earhart landed safely in Ireland. Amelia Earhart had become the first woman to fly solo across the Atlantic.

✗ Half a century later, on June 18, 1983, another woman set out to make history. Sally Ride donned her space suit and her bubble helmet with the ease that you slip on a coat and hat. She climbed aboard the *Challenger* space shuttle with three other astronauts and blasted off into outer space. Sally Ride became the first American woman in space.

Amelia Earhart

Amelia Earhart was born on July 24, 1898, in Atchison, Kansas. While growing up, she liked to experiment with daring stunts. Once, Earhart jumped off her father's barn using an umbrella for a parachute. Another time, she built a roller coaster on the roof of her father's tool shed. Even as a child, Earhart's imagination knew no bounds.

At the age of nineteen, Amelia Earhart discovered flying. She was working as a nurse's aide in a Canadian military hospital. One of her friends was a pilot in the Royal Flying Corps. She spent her free time at a nearby airfield watching him fly. But for Earhart, being only a spectator made her feel like a young athlete left on the bench to watch.

In her early twenties, Earhart began her thrilling and dangerous career as a pilot. The engines of early airplanes were not much bigger than a modern motorcycle engine. In her first two months of flying, Earhart made two crash landings. She was a natural pilot, however. She worked hard to save enough money to buy her own plane in 1922.

When Amelia Earhart took to the air, flying was an endeavor, an effort that was still new and risky. But she pushed herself and the world's flying records to the limit. She set her first record by flying at 14,000 feet (4,200 meters), breaking the women's altitude record.

✔ In 1927, history was made in flying when Charles Lindbergh made the first flight across the Atlantic Ocean. By 1932, Amelia Earhart became the first woman to fly solo across the Atlantic. Her flight brought her international fame. It also inspired her to set one new record after another.

✔✔ In 1935, Earhart became the first person to fly nonstop alone from Honolulu, Hawaii, to the United States mainland. Later, she became the first person to fly nonstop from Los Angeles to Mexico City and from Mexico City to Newark, New Jersey.

Amelia Earhart's daring flights made her a hero to Americans. She was admired and cheered wherever she went. At the time, her accomplishments seemed especially remarkable because of her gender. But Earhart herself deeply believed in gender equality. She believed that women "must earn true respect and equal rights from men by accepting responsibility."

Amelia Earhart's greatest challenge came on May 17, 1937. She had decided to attempt another record-breaking flight—a 27,000-mile (43,200 kilometers) trip around the world. She asked Fred Noonan, an experienced navigator, to join her. Taking off from Oakland, California, they flew to Florida, then to South America, then across the Atlantic to Africa and on to Asia. Finally, they arrived on the island of New Guinea (GIN ee). From there, they faced the most dangerous leg of their journey. They would have to fly 2,556 miles (4,089.6 kilometers) across the Pacific Ocean and then land on tiny Howland Island. On July 2, Earhart and Noonan took off across the Pacific. Somewhere between New Guinea and Howland Island, the plane disappeared. Amelia Earhart was never heard from again.

Sally Ride

Even as a young girl, Sally Ride enjoyed challenges. She competed successfully with neighborhood boys in baseball and football. Once, she threw a ball so hard that it broke the nose of the child next door. At the age of twelve, Ride took up tennis. She was soon winning tournaments. Sally Ride learned early to work hard at everything that she did.

✛ As a young woman, Ride never planned a career in flying. In college, she continued to play tennis. She also gave a great deal of time to serious studying. She spent nine years earning degrees in English, science, and laser physics.

"Then one day in 1977," Ride said, "I read an announcement in the paper that NASA was accepting applications. And all of a sudden, I realized that I wanted to do it. There was no question in my mind." Ride wrote to the National Aeronautics and Space Administration. She expressed her interest in becoming an astronaut. They accepted her immediately, along with seven other women.

By the time Sally Ride joined NASA in 1977, an astronaut had already walked on the moon. Training and scientific know-how were most important for space-age pilots. Ride joined a team of astronauts training for space flights. She worked closely with NASA scientists and other crew members.

After her initial training, Sally Ride was chosen to be the first woman to go up in the *Challenger* space shuttle. As one of two mission specialists aboard the shuttle, Ride made use of two communications satellites and conducted special experiments in space. Ride's extensive training for the STS-7 mission was demanding. Many procedures were practiced again and again. Ride and the other astronauts spent intense hours every day in conditions like those they would face in outer space. There, they would have no weight because gravity would not exist.

> . . . Sally Ride was chosen to be the first woman to go up in the Challenger space shuttle.

As one of the first women astronauts, Sally Ride broke barriers for her gender. Treated with respect by fellow crew members, Ride was simply another good astronaut. She had confidence in the experience and technology of NASA and in her own abilities and training.

Amelia Earhart took off across the huge, lonely Pacific Ocean to achieve a dream. Sally Ride was exposed to an even greater <u>vastness</u> as she blasted off into the endless stretch of emptiness known as outer space. Amelia Earhart and Sally Ride will both go down in history as brave women and pioneers of flight.

Write the answers to the following questions on the lines provided. You may go back to the selection to find an answer.

1. What was the first flight record that Amelia Earhart set?

_____

2. Why didn't Sally Ride do her flying solo?

_____

3. On page 12, reread the two paragraphs that have X's next to them. Underline the sentence that states the main idea in each paragraph.

4. Decide if each statement is true or false. Write *true* or *false* on the lines provided.

_____ a. A spectator plays in a football game.

_____ b. A lot of furniture is needed to fill the vastness of a large living room.

_____ c. Riding a bicycle for the first time is an endeavor most children love.

INTERPRETING FACTS

Not all the questions about a selection are answered directly in the selection. For the following questions, you will have to figure out answers not directly stated in the selection. Write the answers to the questions on the lines provided.

1. Why did Earhart ask Noonan to accompany her on her flight around the world?

_____

2. What effect did Ride's space flight have on future astronaut teams?

_____

3. Reread the paragraph with a cross next to it. Which of the following statements can you infer from the paragraph?
   a. Sally Ride hated to fly.
   b. Sally Ride is very intelligent.
   c. Sally Ride was a bad student.

4. Reread the paragraph with a check mark next to it. Write a sentence describing its main idea.

_____

5. Reread the paragraph with two check marks next to it. Write a sentence describing its main idea.

_____

1. Use the following chart to outline similarities between Amelia Earhart and Sally Ride. In the middle of the chart are general topics. Reread the selection for information on how the women's lives compare. For each topic, write one sentence about each woman. The first one is done for you.

COMPARISONS

Amelia Earhart	Topic	Sally Ride
Earhart was active and daring as a child.	Childhood	Ride was active and competitive as a child.
	Breaking barriers for women	
	Record setting	
	Taking risks	

2. Use the following chart to outline differences between Amelia Earhart and Sally Ride. In the middle of the chart are general topics. Reread the selection to find how the women's lives contrast on these topics. Then write one sentence about each.

CONTRASTS

Amelia Earhart	Topic	Sally Ride
	Beginning of flying career	
	Frontiers of flying	
	Teamwork	

3. Look at the photographs of Amelia Earhart and Sally Ride on pages 12 and 13. In one paragraph, describe the similarities and differences that you see.

_____

_____

_____

▶ Real Life Connections Which quality in these women do you most admire? Tell why.

Classifying

Reading a Science Selection

▶ Background Information

The following selection describes four classes, or types, of objects in space. Each can be found in our solar system. Look over the selection before you read it. Look at the headings that give the names of the four classes. Also look at the boldfaced words in the paragraphs. Following these words, you will find examples of each class. Use headings and boldfaced words to help you understand how the information is organized.

▶ Skill Focus

Sometimes information is organized by **classifying** similar objects or ideas into groups. It is then easier to see similarities and differences among these groups.

You often classify information in your daily life. For example, when you make a budget, you classify expenses. Some costs, such as gasoline, tolls, and parking charges, you classify as transportation expenses. Other costs you classify as housing, food, or medical expenses.

Classifying also helps scientists compare and contrast objects within groups or among groups.

When scientists classify various kinds of rocks, for example, they do so according to how they were formed and the materials they are made of. Each class or type includes rocks that are similar in an important way.

When reading information that explains classes, or types, of objects, notice the headings. They will help you understand how the objects have been divided into classes. As you read, "Objects in Space," ask yourself questions like the following:

1. What is similar about the objects that scientists classify in the same group?
2. How are the objects in one group different from the objects in another group?

▶ Word Clues

When you read a word that you do not know, look for context clues to help you. Context clues are nearby words and phrases that help make the meaning clearer. For example, when you see a word that you do not know in a magazine or newspaper, you often can figure it out by connecting it to words around it that you do know.

Suppose you read:

> The comet flew between other starlike bodies. Its long tail of light shone across the sky.

You can see that a comet is a starlike body with a tail of light that flies across the sky.

Read the sentences below.

> Four classes of objects revolve around the sun. The largest objects that circle the sun are called **planets.**

If you don't know the meaning of the word *revolve,* the word *circle* in the next sentence can help you. The words *revolve* and *circle* are synonyms. To revolve is to circle something.

Use **synonym** context clues to find the meaning of the three underlined words in the selection.

▶ Strategy Tip

As you read the selection, notice in what ways the members of each class are alike. Also notice in what ways the members of each class are different.

Objects in Space

Four classes of objects revolve around the sun. The largest objects that circle the sun are called **planets**. Smaller objects include **asteroids**, **comets**, and **meteoroids**.

Planets

The word *planet* comes from a Greek word meaning "wanderer." A planet is an object in space that revolves around the sun. It produces no light of its own. But sunlight <u>reflects</u> off it. A planet appears to shine in the sky because sunlight bounces off its surface.

Our solar system includes nine planets (*Solar* means "having to do with the sun.") All but two of the planets have moons. Each planet moves around the sun in an oval <u>orbit</u>, or path. The planets that are closer to the sun have shorter orbits than those that are farther away. While each planet moves around the sun, it also <u>rotates</u>, or spins.

The planets are divided into two groups. The planets closest to the sun are called the **inner planets**. These are Mercury, Venus, Earth, and Mars. The planets farthest from the sun are called the outer planets. These are Jupiter, Saturn, Uranus, Neptune, and Pluto.

The Inner Planets The inner planets are similar to Earth in some ways. Like Earth, each is made up of rock and metals. The largest of the inner planets is Earth. It is 12,800 kilometers in diameter. The smallest of the inner planets is Mercury. It is 4,900 kilometers in diameter.

Mercury is a fast-moving planet. It takes tiny Mercury only 88 Earth days to make a trip around the sun. Like Earth's moon, Mercury has many craters. It has no moon of its own, and its atmosphere is extremely thin.

Venus is the brightest of all the planets. In the night sky, it shines even more brightly than a star. Of course, its light is not its own. It is reflected light from the sun.

The atmosphere of Venus is thick. It contains carbon dioxide. This gas keeps heat trapped on Venus. As a result, the temperature on Venus is always over 459°C. The surface of Venus is covered with craters, mountains, and valleys. Venus has no moon.

Earth is often called the "living" planet. This is because Earth is the only planet known to have life. Earth's atmosphere has large amounts of oxygen and clouds of water drops. These gases help make life possible on Earth. Earth has mountains, valleys, craters, and large bodies of water. Earth also has one moon.

Mars is a rocky planet that looks red in space. Large, red, desertlike areas give the planet its color. Mars has a thin atmosphere and icy polar caps. It has two small moons.

The Outer Planets Except for Pluto, the

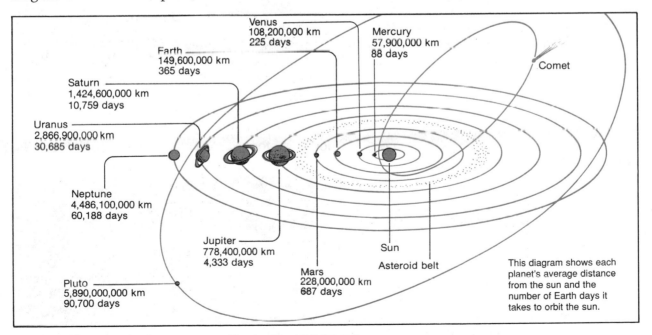

Figure 1. Nine planets plus numerous other bodies orbit the sun.

outer planets are much larger than the inner planets and are made up largely of gases. Most scientists believe that the outer planets have atmospheres that contain large amounts of hydrogen and helium, as well as small amounts of frozen ammonia and methane. The centers of these planets may contain heavy liquids.

Jupiter is twice the size of all the other planets put together. It is 142,800 kilometers in diameter. Colorful clouds surround this large planet, and 16 moons circle it. Jupiter seems to have a huge red area on its surface. Scientists have named it the Great Red Spot. The spot is so large that three Earths could fit side by side across it. The Great Red Spot seems to be a giant gas storm caused by new gases rising from deep inside the planet.

Saturn is one of the most beautiful planets. It is surrounded by seven rings. Scientists believe these rings are made of billions of rock and ice bits revolving around the planet like tiny moons. Saturn has 17 true moons.

Uranus and **Neptune** are called the twin planets. They look alike and are about the same size. Uranus, however, has many rings and at least 15 moons. Neptune has no rings

Which planet has polar ice caps and two small moons?

and eight known moons. Because Neptune is farther from the sun, it is colder than Uranus.

Pluto is the planet that is farthest from the sun. Sometimes, though, its unusual orbit brings it closer to the sun than Neptune. Pluto is unlike the other outer planets. It is made up of rocky, earthlike materials, not gases. And it is not a large planet. In fact, with a diameter of 2,284 kilometers, Pluto is smaller than Mercury. Pluto has one moon.

Asteroids

Like the inner planets, asteroids are made up of chunks of rock and metal. However, asteroids are smaller than planets. Some are only about one kilometer in diameter. Others are several hundred kilometers in diameter.

Our solar system contains thousands of asteroids. The number now known and named is over 5,000. Most move around the sun in the gap between Mars and Jupiter. This gap is called the **asteroid belt.** A few asteroids move around the sun in oval orbits.

The larger asteroids have been given names. Ceres, the largest, is about 1,030 kilometers in diameter. It is one of the asteroids that moves in an orbit outside the asteroid belt.

Comets

A comet is a spectacular sight. The head, or **coma,** of a comet is made up of frozen gases and bits of rock and dust. As a comet nears the sun, a bright tail develops behind the head.

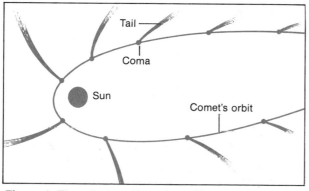

Figure 2. The tail of a comet grows longer as it nears the sun.

Figure 3. Barringer Crater in Arizona is 1.3 kilometers across and 200 meters deep.

Energy given off by the sun pushes material away from the coma to form the tail. The tail grows as the comet nears the sun. Most comas are only a few kilometers across.

Only a few comets are seen regularly. This is because most comets follow extremely long orbits. Some take thousands of years to complete an orbit around the sun. The most famous comet is **Halley's Comet.** It passes Earth every 76 years. It last appeared in 1986.

Meteoroids

Meteoroids are rock and metal objects that speed around the sun. Most are no bigger than a grain of sand. A few are larger and may weigh many tons.

Every now and then, a meteoroid enters Earth's atmosphere. When this happens, it is called a **meteor,** or "shooting star." Earth's atmosphere causes the meteor to burn and glow. Groups of meteors entering Earth's atmosphere together are called meteor showers.

Most meteors burn up completely while passing through Earth's atmosphere. A few are large enough to make it to Earth's surface. The rocky material that hits Earth is called a **meteorite.** A few large meteorites have made craters on Earth. **Barringer Meteorite** made a crater in Arizona 1.3 kilometers wide.

RECALLING FACTS

Write the answers to questions 1 through 8 on the lines provided. You may go back to the selection to find an answer.

1. What do a planet and an asteroid have in common?

_____

_____

2. How are planets different from asteroids?

_____

3. Name two ways in which a planet moves.

_____

_____

4. What kinds of objects in space have moons?

_____

5. What is the asteroid belt?

_____

_____

6. What pushes material away from a comet's head, or coma, to form its tail?

_____

7. Why are comets seen so seldom?

_____

_____

8. What is the difference between a meteoroid and a meteor?

_____

_____

9. Fill in the space next to the word that completes each sentence.

a. A mirror _____ the image of the person looking into it.
   ‖ rotates   ‖ revolves   ‖ reflects

b. Wheels, tops, and planets _____.
   ‖ reflect   ‖ rotate   ‖ orbit

c. Some human-made satellites can _____ the earth in less than one hour.
   ‖ orbit   ‖ reflect   ‖ vapor

d. Many planets have one or more _____ that orbit around them.
   ‖ meteors   ‖ comets   ‖ moons

e. The distance through the center of a planet from one side to the other side is called its_____.
   ‖ orbit   ‖ atmosphere   ‖ diameter

Not all the questions about a selection are answered directly in the selection. For the following questions, you will have to figure out answers not directly stated in the selection. Write the answers to the questions on the lines provided.

1. Why does the word *wanderer* apply as much to comets, asteroids, and meteoroids as it does to planets?

_____

2. What is the main difference between a planet, an asteroid, and a meteoroid?

_____

3. Some scientists call Pluto an Earthlike planet and classify it with Mercury, Venus, Earth, and Mars. Explain why.

_____

_____

4. Ikeya-Seki approached the sun in 1965. Its tail was extremely bright. To what group does this object belong?

_____

5. In your reading and in the pictures, you can see the planets' oval orbits. How would you describe the meaning of oval?

_____

SKILL FOCUS

Use details from the selection about each class of objects in space to complete the chart below. The first part has been done for you.

	Materials	Size	Movement and Other Characteristics
INNER PLANETS **Mercury, Venus, Earth, Mars**	Rock and metal	4,990–12,800 km in diameter	Move in oval orbit; rotate; all but two have moons; produce no light
OUTER PLANETS **Jupiter, Saturn, Uranus, Neptune, Pluto**			
ASTEROIDS			
COMETS			
METEOROIDS			

▶ **Real Life Connections** Would you accept an invitation to travel through space? Tell why or why not.

Mathematical Terms and Symbols

__ Reading a Mathematics Selection __

▶ Background Information

As you read the following selection, pay close attention to the diagrams. They will help you understand the special meanings of certain words. Also study the symbols that represent some of the ideas. These symbols are shortened ways of writing mathematical concepts.

▶ Skill Focus

When reading many types of material, you may come across terms, or words that are used in a special way. The words may have meanings that you know when they are used in an ordinary situation. However, when they are used in a special situation, they may have different meanings.

Look at the following words. Most of them have familiar meanings that you know from using them in your daily life. In mathematics, they have different meanings, though some are similar to meanings that you already know.

• **Point:** We ask people to "get the point," meaning to understand our meaning. We speak of "a point of time," meaning a specific time, such as 3:15 P.M. In mathematics, however, a point is invisible; it has no size and no dimensions.

• **Line:** In life, we talk about a line on a football field, a line on a page, a line of people at the movies or in a store. In mathematics, a line is many points placed next to each other; it goes on forever.

• **Plane:** A plane is a flat space. In life, we usually refer to planes as specific things— a table top, a street, a floor. In mathematics, a plane has length and width but no height; it goes on forever.

• **Intersect:** Many of us use the word "intersection" every day for a place where two or more streets or highways cross each other. In the same way, lines and planes can cross, or intersect.

• **Perpendicular:** When lines or planes intersect and form square corners, they are perpendicular. The doors and walls of rooms are perpendicular to their floors. The walls of buildings are perpendicular to sidewalks and streets.

• **Parallel:** Lines on a plane that do not intersect are parallel to each other. The tracks for trains run parallel, but sometimes intersect when the trains change their direction. In mathematics, parallel lines never intersect.

▶ Word Clues

When reading the following selection, look for these important words: *point, line, plane, intersect, perpendicular,* and *parallel.* The diagrams should help you understand these words as they apply to mathematics. Be sure also to pay special attention to the symbols that stand for special words.

▶ Strategy Tip

Be sure that you understand each idea before you go on to the next one. If you fail to understand one idea, others that follow it may be confusing. In mathematics, you must pay attention to logical connections at every point.

Reading Mathematical Terms and Symbols

To study geometry, you must understand three important terms. They are *point, line,* and *plane*. A **point** has no dimensions. It cannot be seen. It has no size. A point is shown by a dot and named with a capital letter. This is the symbol for point *A*.

•A

A **line** is many, many points placed next to each other. When a line is drawn, it looks as if it has a beginning and an end. But the arrows show that it goes on forever.

A line can be named with a small letter. This is line *s*. It is written *line s*.

A line can also be named using two points. A capital letter is used to name each of the two points on the line. The two points can be placed anywhere on this line.

This is line *AB*. The symbol for line *AB* is $\overleftrightarrow{AB}$.

Just like a line, a **plane** goes on and on. It never ends. It has length and width but no height. A plane is also named with a capital letter. This is plane *M*. It is written *plane M*. The four-sided figure shows that it is a plane.

Each side goes on forever. When you see this figure, you should remember that the sides do not mean that the plane ends. The capital letter that names the plane is in the lower right corner of the figure.

✔ When two lines cross, they **intersect.** Two lines intersect in a point. This is line *x* and line *y* intersecting in point O.

Two lines can intersect and form square corners. The lines are **perpendicular** to each other. Line *l* is perpendicular to line *m*. The symbol for showing that line *l* is perpendicular to line *m* is $l \perp m$.

Sometimes two lines never intersect. The distance between them is always the same. When two lines never intersect, they are said to be **parallel** to each other. Line *a* is parallel to line *b*. The symbol to show that line *a* is parallel to line *b* is $a \| b$.

A line can also intersect a plane. A line and a plane intersect in a point. This is *RS* intersecting plane *P* at point *L*. The dotted line shows the part of the line that is behind the plane.

Two planes can also intersect. When planes intersect, they always intersect in a line. This shows plane *S* and plane *T* intersecting along *CD*.

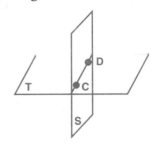

RECALLING FACTS

Complete the following sentences by writing the correct words on the lines provided.

1. What are three important terms in geometry?

   _____, _____, _____

2. When two lines cross, they _____.

3. Two lines that never intersect are _____ to each other.

4. Two lines that intersect and form square corners are _____ to each other.

5. Reread the paragraph with a check mark next to it. Draw a line under the sentence that states the main idea.

6. Write a meaning for each of the following phrases.

   intersecting lines _____

   _____

   parallel lines _____

   _____

   perpendicular lines _____

   _____

INTERPRETING FACTS

Not all the questions about a selection are answered directly in the selection. For the following questions, you will have to figure out answers not directly stated in the story. Write the answers to the following questions.

1. Could two planes intersect in a point? Why or why not?

   _____

   _____

2. Could two lines intersect in two points?

   _____

3. Write the words *plane, point,* and *line* in order from the one that takes the least space to the one that takes the most space.

   _____, _____, _____

A. Write the name or symbol for each figure.

1.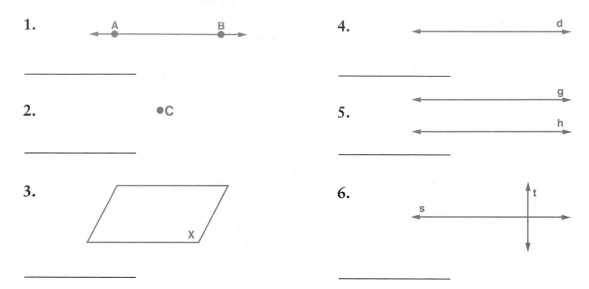

_____

2.   •C

_____

3.

_____

4.

_____

5.

_____

6.

_____

B. Draw a diagram for each name or symbol.

1. point X

2. $\overleftrightarrow{AB}$

3. line m

4. plane D

5. $a \| b$

6. $g \perp h$

7. line CD and line ST intersecting in point H

8. line XY intersecting plane M in point C

▶ **Real Life Connections** Describe something around you that is perpendicular.

Vowel Diphthongs

Say the words *oil* and *boy* to yourself. Listen to their vowel sound. The letters *oi* and *oy* have the same vowel sound. When this vowel sound appears at the beginning or in the middle of a word, it is usually spelled *oi*. When this same sound is at the end of a word, it is spelled *oy*. This sound is called a **vowel diphthong.**

Read the sentences below. Choose a word from the list to complete each sentence. Write the word on the line.

coin	annoy	broil
enjoy	coil	noise

1. Some children _____ their parents by breaking their toys.

2. This vine will _____ around the tree.

3. Cars in heavy traffic often make _____ by honking their horns.

4. Mr. Larsen is planning to _____ the hamburgers over charcoal.

5. Joe and Ann _____ going to hockey games.

6. Numismatics, or _____ collecting, is a popular hobby.

Say the words *out* and *cow* to yourself. Listen to their vowel sound. The letters *ou* and *ow* have the same vowel sound. This sound is also called a **vowel diphthong.**

Read the sentences below. Choose a word from the list to complete each sentence. Write the word on the line.

town	cloud	crowd	shout
pouch	blouse	plow	brow

1. The cowhands rode off in a _____ of dust.

2. Heather wore her blue _____ with her gray skirt.

3. A _____ is larger than a village but smaller than a city.

4. In earlier times, an ox was used to pull a _____ .

5. The female kangaroo carries her young in her _____ .

6. A large _____ gathered at the scene of the fire.

7. Neil wiped the sweat from his _____ .

8. Kerry tried to _____ to the other players on her team.

Vowel-Consonant Combinations

The vowel-consonant combinations *aw* and *al* and the vowels *au* have the same sound you hear in the words *claw, bald,* and *auto.* The vowel sound in all three words is the same, but the letters that stand for the sound are different.

Read the sentences below. Choose a word from the list to complete each sentence. Write the word on the line.

hawk	thaw	because	caught	fault	salt	ball
yawn	crawl	sauce	dawn	false	paw	gnaw
taught	pause	bald	haul	straw	halt	law

1. Tired people often _____.

2. Last year Ms. White _____ geometry.

3. It is not healthful for people to put too much _____ on their food.

4. Carol _____ four fish within a short time.

5. An answer that is not true is _____.

6. The sun rises at _____.

7. Mr. Barlaz poured _____ over the spaghetti.

8. Most babies _____ before they learn to walk.

9. It is Robert's _____ that we are late for dinner.

10. Althea left the party early _____ she was tired.

11. The hot sun made the ice start to _____.

12. My cat hurt its _____ while running on the gravel driveway.

13. Ruth was told to _____ before reading the story.

14. My grandfather is _____.

15. This _____ has a very sharp beak.

16. Ming's new truck can _____ our glass to the recycling plant.

17. My large _____ hat will protect my face from sunburn.

18. The horse will _____ if you pull on the reins.

19. The players kicked the _____.

20. After dinner, our dog would _____ the bones that we gave him.

21. To drive when you are drunk is against the _____.

Syllables

One way to help you pronounce long words is to divide the words into syllables. Then pronounce each syllable until you can say the whole word. There are several different ways of deciding how a word should be divided.

Guide 1: Compound Words

One of the easiest guides to use in dividing words is the one that is used with a compound word. Because a compound word is made up of two words, it must have at least two syllables. Always divide a compound word into syllables by separating it between the two smaller words first. If one or even both of the smaller words in a compound word have more than one syllable, it may be necessary to use another guide. However, you can pronounce most compound words if you divide them into two words.

sailboat   sail   boat

Read each of the following compound words. Divide the word into two syllables by writing each of the two smaller words separately on the line to the right of the compound word.

1. weekday ———————————
2. seaweed ———————————
3. flashlight ———————————
4. driftwood ———————————
5. grassland ———————————
6. withdraw ———————————

7. bathtub ———————————
8. baseball ———————————
9. windshield ———————————
10. drumstick ———————————
11. highchair ———————————
12. background ———————————

Guide 2: Words with Double Consonants

Another guide that you may use is for words with double consonants. Divide the word into two syllables between the two consonants and read each syllable.

tennis   ten   nis

Divide the following two-syllable words into syllables. Write each syllable separately on the line to the right of the word.

1. raccoon ———————————
2. penny ———————————
3. lesson ———————————
4. slipper ———————————
5. lettuce ———————————
6. kitten ———————————
7. sudden ———————————

8. rabbit ———————————
9. tunnel ———————————
10. splatter ———————————
11. muffin ———————————
12. gossip ———————————
13. hammer ———————————
14. traffic ———————————

Stated or Unstated Main Idea

When you read a textbook or reference book for information, the main idea of each paragraph will often be stated in a sentence. The rest of the paragraph will contain the supporting details that give additional information about the main idea.

Sometimes the main idea of a paragraph is not stated in one of the sentences. The information given in the paragraph will help you to **infer**, or figure out, the main idea yourself. To do this, you need to ask yourself what the paragraph is about. Then think of a sentence that summarizes this idea.

Read the following selection from beginning to end to become familiar with the content. Then reread each paragraph. Think about whether the main idea in each paragraph is stated or unstated.

Shooting for the Moon

1. Dr. Mae Jemison will never forget the day of September 12, 1992. She leads an adventure-filled life, but this was surely one of her most exciting days. "I had this big smile on my face," said Jemison. "I was so excited. This is what I had wanted to do for a very long time." Jemison was aboard shuttle mission STS-47 Spacelab, a cooperative mission to outer space between the United States and Japan.

2. Space travel is exciting, but in some ways it only emphasizes what a small planet Earth is. "The first thing I saw was Chicago. I looked out the window and there it was," she said about seeing her hometown from the shuttle. "I looked over at one point, and there was Somalia.

3. "Space is so meaningful to Earth. The Third World will be the [part of our world to gain the most from] space technology," she said, because old-fashioned telephone lines and electrical generators won't be necessary. She thinks that the "space age" will enable the Third World to skip over the "industrial age."

4. Jemison is a physician, chemical engineer, and former astronaut. When she was in medical school, Jemison studied social medicine in Cuba. Later, she practiced medicine with rural Kenyan villagers and Cambodians who had escaped to Thailand after the fall of Phnom Penh to a communist government. She also worked as a Peace Corps medical officer in Sierra Leone and Liberia. Born in 1957, Jemison is still young, but she has already done much to help people all over the world.

5. Jemison insists, however, that she does not do what she does for the good of other people. "I don't believe in [doing good just to be unselfish]," she said. "I've gotten much more out of what I have done than the people I was supposed to be helping." Jemison was in the camp in Thailand for refugees, people who left their countries to escape war and find freedom. "I learned more about medicine there than I could have in a lifetime somewhere else," she said.

6. Only a handful of women have gone up in space, and Jemison was the first African American woman to do so. However, she does not like her ethnicity to be highlighted in her work. "When I'm asked about the relevance to black people of what I do, I take that as an [insult]. It presupposes that black people have never been involved in exploring

the heavens, but this is not so. Ancient African empires—Mali, Songhay, Egypt—had scientists and astronomers.

7. "The fact is that space and its resources belong to all of us, not to any one group," Jemison emphasizes. "We need more African Americans and Latinos in the field. We need biologists, who can put together parts of experiments; chemists for rocket fuel; and even lawyers, who one day might write the contracts to determine who has mineral rights to mine the moon. If we're not there from the beginning, helping to determine what happens to these resources, we'll have no say in how they are to be used."

8. Jemison chose some very special objects to take with her in the shuttle: "An Alvin Ailey American Dance Theater poster, an Alpha Kappa Alpha banner, a flag that had flown over the Organization of African Unity, and [important writings] from Chicago's DuSable Museum of African American History and the Chicago public-school system." She explained, "I wanted everyone to know that space belongs to all of us. There is science in dance and art in science. It belongs to everyone. I'm not the first or the only African American woman who had the skills and talent to become an astronaut. I had the opportunity. All people have produced scientists and astronomers."

9. When poet Nikki Giovanni interviewed Jemison in 1993 after her shuttle mission, she asked her what her ideal space trip would be. Jemison replied, "Me in a clear bubble floating through the galaxy . . . shooting for the moon." When asked who she would bring with her, she said, "Sneeze, my cat. I think I'd like to have Sneeze. He came with me from Africa, so he's used to flying. Then if some aliens came by and invited me to another galaxy—well, look for me on *Unsolved Mysteries*. I'm gone."

For each paragraph in the selection, if the main idea is stated, write *stated* on the line. If the main idea is unstated, choose a main idea from the sentences below and write the letter on the line.

a. Jemison's cat Sneeze came with her from Africa, so he's used to flying.

b. Space is particularly meaningful to the Third World.

c. Black people have always explored space.

d. Jemison worked as a Peace Corps officer in Sierra Leone and Liberia.

e. Old-fashioned telephone lines and electrical generators won't be necessary in the Third World.

f. On September 12, 1992, Jemison reached her goal of going up in a shuttle.

g. Jemison is always ready for another adventure.

h. Lawyers can one day write contracts to determine who has mineral rights to mine the moon.

i. More African Americans and Latinos are needed in space so that they will have a say in what happens.

Paragraph 1 ——————   Paragraph 6 ——————

Paragraph 2 ——————   Paragraph 7 ——————

Paragraph 3 ——————   Paragraph 8 ——————

Paragraph 4 ——————   Paragraph 9 ——————

Paragraph 5 ——————

Now go back to each paragraph that has a stated main idea and underline the sentence with the main idea.

The Dictionary

In a dictionary, you may find several pages of words that all begin with the same first three letters. To find a word on these pages, you will need to use the fourth letter of a word. For example, the word *collar* is listed before the word *color* because *l* comes before *o* in the alphabet. When words begin with the same three letters, they are arranged in alphabetical order according to the fourth letter of the words.

On the numbered lines, write each set of words below in alphabetical order according to the first four letters in each word. Cross out each word in the list after you write it.

beam	1. _____		stole	1. _____
beagle	2. _____		stove	2. _____
bear	3. _____		stomach	3. _____
beauty	4. _____		stoop	4. _____
beat	5. _____		store	5. _____
beach	6. _____		stodgy	6. _____
beaver	7. _____		stop	7. _____
bean	8. _____		stoke	8. _____
bead	9. _____		stone	9. _____
beak	10. _____		stock	10. _____

At the top of each dictionary page are two words in boldfaced type. These words are called **guide words.** Guide words help you find, easily and quickly, the entry words—the words for which the dictionary gives definitions. They tell you the first entry word on the page and the last entry word on the page. All the other entry words on the page come between these two words in alphabetical order.

Below is a pair of guide words that might appear on a dictionary page. Following them is a list of entry words. If the entry would be on the same page as the guide words, write *yes* next to the word. If the entry would appear on an earlier page, write *before.* If the entry would appear on a later page, write *after.*

parboil / parson

1. parrot	_____		7. pastry	_____
2. part	_____		8. pardon	_____
3. parcel	_____		9. paragraph	_____
4. pass	_____		10. parlor	_____
5. parasol	_____		11. Paris	_____
6. parent	_____		12. part	_____

13. parallel _____   16. pare _____

14. party _____   17. particle _____

15. parade _____   18. parole _____

In a dictionary, an entry word and all the information about it is called an **entry.** The entry word always appears in boldfaced type. If the entry word has more than one syllable, it is divided into syllables to show where the word can be divided at the end of a line of writing. The entry word is followed by a **respelling** of the word in parentheses. The respelling shows you how to say the word. The part-of-speech label follows the respelling. The labels are usually abbreviated as follows: *adj.* for adjective, *adv.* for adverb, *conj.* for conjunction, *interj.* for interjection, *n.* for noun, *prep.* for preposition, *pron.* for pronoun, and *v.* for verb.

The meanings of an entry word are arranged according to parts of speech. For example, if an entry has noun meanings, all the noun meanings are grouped together and numbered following the *n.* label. Any meanings the word may have for any other part of speech are numbered and placed after the abbreviated part-of-speech label. When an entry has only one meaning for any part of speech, the definition is not numbered. Many words that appear in dictionary entries are synonyms for the entry word.

At the end of some entries are idioms. An **idiom** is a group of words that has a meaning different from the meaning the words have by themselves.

Use the dictionary entry below to answer the following questions.

> **name** (nām) *n.* 1 a word or words by which a person, animal, thing, or place is known: title [Grace, Lopez, Wyoming, and poodle are *names.*] 2 a word or words used instead of the real name, sometimes in order to insult [They were mean and called him *names,* such as "liar" and "cheat."] 3 reputation [Guard your good *name.*] ◆*v.* **named, nam'ing** 1 to give a name to [He *named* the child after her mother.] 2 to tell the name or names of [Can you *name* all the Presidents?] 3 to refer to; mention [to *name* an example]. 4 to choose for a certain position; appoint [She was *named* president of the company.] 5 to fix or set, as a date for a meeting, a price, etc. —**in the name of, 1** for the sake of [*in the name of* good sense]. **2** by the authority of [Open *in the name of* the law!] —**to one's name,** belonging to one.

1. What is the entry word? _____

2. Write the respelling. _____

3. How many noun meanings follow the part-of-speech label *n*? _____

4. How many verb meanings follow the part-of-speech label *v*? _____

5. Write the first verb meaning. _____

6. Write the second idiom. _____

7. Write the two synonyms given for the entry word as a noun. _____, _____.

8. Write the idiom that has the same meaning as the underlined words in the following sentence.
   I ordered the equipment <u>by the authority of</u> my supervisor. _____

Reading Help Wanted Ads

Help wanted ads are found in the classified section of the newspaper. The classified section of the newspaper lists advertisements for all kinds of things arranged by subject. In the help wanted listings, ads for the same kind of job are listed together. Each ad begins with a job title or a descriptive heading that identifies the job. Sometimes a key word in the upper left-hand corner of the advertisement tells the kind of job being offered. Ads are listed in alphabetical order by job title or key word.

Most help wanted ads give the job seeker a variety of information. In addition to the job title, a help wanted ad may describe the skills needed for the job. It may state that previous experience, or former work in the same type of job, is required. An ad tells how to apply for the job. Other information, such as salary, or pay, may be included.

Because help wanted ads must give a lot of information in a small amount of space, abbreviations, or shortened forms of words, are used. For example, *exp* is the abbreviation for the word *experience*. Sometimes the abbreviations contain the first few letters of the word; sometimes the abbreviations use only consonants. If you use context clues, you can usually figure out the abbreviations.

Sometimes an ad may state that the company requires a résumé. A résumé is a sheet of written information about yourself and your work experience that you make available to a company. If the company wants to meet you after reading your résumé, someone at the company will contact you for an interview.

Examine the help wanted ads below.

AIRLINE	AIRLINE/TRAVEL	AIRLINE	AIRLINE Station/Operations

AIRLINE
FLIGHT ATTENDANTS
Major airlines looking for college grads. No exp necessary. Must be willing to move to Atlanta or Dallas. Interviews 9–5 Sept 2 at 616 N. Orchard Ave. See Cheryl Barnes.

AIRLINE
GROUND PERSONNEL
Be a reservation or ticket agent at airport. Weekends or evenings 11 PM–7 AM shift. Sal up to $25,000 dep on exp. Call 555-4597 wkdys.

AIRLINE/TRAVEL
Reservation/
    ticket agents   to $25,000
Secretaries/typists   to $20,000
Baggage handlers   to $17,000
Aircraft mechanics   to $26,000

NEAR & FAR Agency will find the right job for you. 30 E. Orange St. 555-8000.

AIRLINE
PILOTS
wanted
Minimum 5 years exp in commercial flying. Flights to Europe. Send resume and sal requirements to:
OVERSEAS AIRWAYS
105 Park Place
San Jose, CA 95126

AIRLINE Secy-Ludwig Airport
Must type 60 wpm and know DOS. P/T Mon–Thurs 8AM–11AM. Call Jonathan Chong for appointment 555-8188.

AIRLINE Station/Operations
Manager
Exp in all phases of airport operations. Excellent salary. Call 555-0433.

A. Read the abbreviations from the ads. On the line next to each abbreviation, write the word it stands for. If necessary, use context clues from the ads.

1. grads _____
2. sal _____
3. dep _____
4. wkdys _____

5. yrs _____
6. secy _____
7. wpm _____
8. P/T _____

B. Use the information in the ads to answer each question.

1. Which job requires someone to run an airport? _____

2. Which job requires moving to another city? _____

3. Which two jobs are for someone who likes to travel by airplane to different places?

_____

4. Which job would be for someone who wants to work a few hours a day?

_____

5. Which job pays up to $17,000? _____

6. Which two jobs require previous experience? _____

7. Which two telephone numbers would you call for information about a job as a secretary?

_____

8. How would you apply for the job of flight attendant? _____

_____

9. What is the job title for a reservation or ticket agent at an airport? _____

10. What is the location of the part-time job for an airline secretary? _____

11. Which ad asks the applicants to tell how much money they would like to make?

_____

12. What skill would you need to apply for the airline secretary job? _____

13. What are two requirements for people who want to apply for the flight attendant's job?

_____

14. Why might some people not want to apply for the ground personnel job?

_____

15. Where can you go to find out about a job involved with airlines or travel if you're not

certain exactly what you're best suited for? _____

16. What do you think an aircraft mechanic does? _____

17. The ground personnel job pays up to $25,000. Who do you think could earn that salary—

a person with no experience or a person who has been a ticket agent? _____

_____

Theme

Reading a Literature Selection

▶ **Background Information**

When you start a new class, get a new teacher, or join a club or team, you have to deal with new people and new ways of doing things. On a job, you often face changes—new work, new bosses, new co-workers. As our world grows smaller, more and more people from different countries and races come together and have to get along with each other.

Learning how to get along in a new situation can be one of life's hardest lessons. In this story, a young Japanese American girl tries to find her roots in Japan. She struggles with customs that are difficult for her to learn, such as wearing a kimono, hiding her feelings, and arranging flowers.

▶ **Skill Focus**

Theme is the meaning or message in a story. In most stories, the author does not directly state the theme. Instead, the reader must think about the characters and plot to infer, or figure out, the theme. A story's title might also give a clue about the theme.

In a story with a theme, characters often experience a change of attitude that makes us see a truth about life. We put ourselves in their place and learn a lesson by sharing their experiences.

In a similar way, the plots of such stories, by describing the problems that people face, allow us to see how the characters deal with these challenges. Their struggles help us gain a deeper understanding of the values that make life worthwhile. Without telling us directly, the author lets us see behavior that can bring maturity, self-respect, and happiness.

The following questions will help you figure out the theme of a story.

1. What does the main character learn about himself or herself or others by the end of the story?
2. What does the title of the story mean? How is it appropriate?
3. What is the author's message?

▶ **Word Clues**

Read the sentence below. Look for context clues that explain the underlined word.

> Keiko was shy, not <u>outspoken</u> like Tomi.

If you don't know the meaning of the word *outspoken*, the word *shy* can help you. *Outspoken* and *shy* are antonyms, or words that are opposite in meaning from one another. *Outspoken* means "not shy."

Look for **antonym** context clues to find the meaning of the three underlined words in the selection.

▶ **Strategy Tip**

As you read, think about the customs that Tomi must learn, especially flower arranging. See if you can figure out how the key to arranging flowers helps Tomi adjust to other customs. Use the questions to help you infer the story's theme.

A Simple Arrangement

"I give up!" Tomi cried. She threw the spray of yellow flowers to the floor.

Her cousin Keiko blinked her eyes in amazement. Keiko was shy, not outspoken like Tomi. Tomi had never learned to keep her feelings to herself as Japanese girls are taught to do. Keiko did not know what to say.

"I'm sorry I shouted," Tomi said. She bent to pick up the flowers. "It's just that I'll never learn to arrange flowers."

"Yes you will," Keiko said gently. "It is the Japanese way."

"But that's just it!" Tomi burst out again. "I'm not Japanese. I'm American. I was born in California, and I lived there all my life until now. My parents may be Japanese, and I may look Japanese, but that just makes it harder. Everyone expects me to do things the Japanese way. But I can't!"

All the anger Tomi had felt these last few months came rushing out. She hadn't wanted to come to Japan in the first place. But when her grandparents had invited her to spend a year in Japan, Tomi's father said it was a fine idea. Once Father made up his mind, it was no use arguing. The word of a Japanese father is not questioned—even in America!

Once she was in Japan, Tomi had honestly tried to be the sort of girl her grandparents wanted her to be. She had worked very hard at doing well in school and at becoming adept in flower arranging. But her hands seemed clumsy working with flowers. She felt that she did everything wrong.

"I think you are very lucky to be both Japanese and American," Keiko said. "You have two homes and two languages. That is something special."

"You're the one that's lucky," said Tomi. "You belong here. I don't."

Tomi cut three flowers from the spray and put them in the bowl as she had seen Mr. Tanaka, her teacher, do many times. She had cut the stems in the Japanese way so that they were three different lengths. The flower with the short stem represented earth. The tall flower stood for heaven. The medium length flower stood for human beings, who link heaven and earth.

Once heaven, human beings, and earth were in harmony, the flower arrangement succeeded. An arrangement was supposed to have proportion. But Tomi's flowers looked unbalanced. The design was all wrong. It was supposed to be so simple to achieve a pleasing arrangement of flowers. Why couldn't she learn how to do it? Would Tomi ever be able to please her grandparents?

Tomi sighed. "I hoped I could make a pretty flower arrangement for the party tonight," she said sadly. "It would make Grandmother so happy."

Keiko's eyes danced at the thought of the celebration. "Are you going to wear the kimono that Grandmother and Grandfather gave you when you arrived here?" she asked. "It is so beautiful."

"I know it is," Tomi said. "But I wouldn't feel right wearing it." The long, flowing kimonos that many Japanese women wear on special occasions looked lovely on them. Kimonos were really much prettier than Western clothes, Tomi thought. But she would make a fool of herself in a kimono. Kimonos are narrow, so you have to take short steps with your knees close together. Otherwise, the kimono will flap open. Tomi was sure she would forget about walking properly. She would look clumsy and silly. It was better not even to try.

"It's time for me to go home and help my family get ready for tonight," Keiko said. She got to her feet and crossed the room in quick, graceful steps.

Tomi felt a stab of envy as she watched her cousin. Keiko would wear a kimono to the family gathering tonight. Keiko would know the right things to do and say, too. Manners are much more casual in America, Tomi thought. Here it is important to do everything just right. Tomi always seemed to do everything wrong.

After Keiko had gone, Tomi felt tears in her eyes. She thought about her family back in California. More than anything, she wanted to feel like part of a family again. But she would never be accepted here, not when she couldn't even arrange a few flowers!

Tomi picked up the flowers again. The

words of Mr. Tanaka came back to her: "Arranging flowers is a simple thing, but it cannot be done unless your heart is <u>serene</u>."

"That must be my problem," Tomi thought. "My heart is anything but serene. I feel tense and anxious. My heart is not at peace."

Just then, Grandmother came into the room. Her arms were filled with packages of food for the party.

"I smell rice burning!" Grandmother said.

Oh dear! Tomi suddenly remembered that she had put rice on the stove to cook. She had hoped to please Grandmother by making the evening rice, but she had forgotten it. The water must have boiled away. The rice would be black and burned. Couldn't she do anything right?

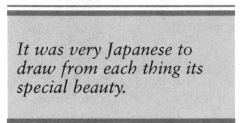

It was very Japanese to draw from each thing its special beauty.

Tomi fled from the house. Once she was in the garden, she let the tears fall. She sank into the soft moss and put her face in her hands. She had never felt so lost and alone.

It was very quiet. Her sobbing slowed, and she wiped her eyes. She looked around the garden. How beautiful it was! A pine branch was reflected in the little pond. The cherry tree was a huge ball of white blossoms.

It was a tiny garden, yet every inch of it was a delight. Her grandfather had planned it that way, she knew. It was very Japanese to draw from each thing its special beauty. The Japanese found joy in the smallest things. Things as simple as the moon rising or a bird singing were treated as treasures.

Tomi had been in the garden many times, but she had always been too busy to notice how carefully planned yet simple it was. Few other Americans would have noticed it either, she thought. Americans moved too fast. They didn't have time to watch a flower bud.

Perhaps she had been trying to move too fast, Tomi thought. She had been in such a great hurry to learn everything right away. If she moved a bit more slowly, perhaps she would find the beauty in simple things. The Japanese knew there was comfort in beauty. I'm lucky to be Japanese, Tomi thought. Lucky to be here. Lucky just to be alive!

Tomi hugged that warm feeling to her as she went back inside. Her heart was full of joy as she slipped off her shoes at the door.

"Where is the pot I burned, Grandmother?" she asked. "I want to scrub it clean."

"I've done it for you," said Grandmother.

Tomi waited for her to say more about the burned rice. Tomi had acted like an American again, wasting food! But her grandmother just went on with the preparations for dinner. She knows I can't help being what I am, Tomi thought. I am American, too.

Relieved, she picked up the yellow flowers again. This time her hands moved easily as she placed the stems in the bowl. She arranged the flowers slowly and with love for their beauty.

She stepped back to see the results. It was a very simple arrangement. There were just three stems. But it looked natural, almost as if the spray grew right out of the bowl. It was beautiful and right and Japanese.

That night, Tomi put on the silk kimono that her grandparents had given her. It was as blue as the sky and had peach blossoms scattered across it. The long, flowing sleeves fell almost to the floor.

That evening, Tomi's steps were not always as tiny as they should have been. But most of the time she remembered how to walk, and she knew she looked right. Like Keiko, Tomi helped make the passing moments of the evening beautiful.

Grandmother said nothing about the flowers. Grandfather didn't mention the kimono. But Tomi saw the glow of pride in their eyes. She felt their love reach out and wrap her like a cloak.

In the garden, the wind blew among the cherry trees, scattering the white flowers like confetti against the moon. Tomi watched each petal fall through the air of the peaceful Japanese evening.

RECALLING FACTS

1. Why did Tomi go to Japan?

_____

2. What is the relationship between Tomi and Keiko?

_____

3. **a.** How are Tomi and Keiko alike?

_____

   b. How are they different?

_____

_____

_____

4. Why did Keiko say Tomi was lucky?

_____

5. Why did Tomi go to Japan?

_____

6. Why did Tomi run to the garden and cry?

_____

_____

7. Why didn't Tomi want to wear a kimono?

_____

8. What do the shortest flowers in a Japanese arrangement represent? The tallest? The medium size?

_____

_____

9. Draw a line to match each word with its meaning.

proportion   trained

   adept   calm and peaceful

   serene   balance of parts

INTERPRETING FACTS

1. If Keiko visited the United States, what customs and traits might she have to get used to?

_____

_____

2. How is Tomi changing as a result of her time in Japan?

_____

_____

3. How would you describe the grandparents' attitude toward Tomi at the end?

_____

4. Mr. Tanaka told Tomi that flower arranging is done with different lengths of stems and a serene heart. Part of this statement is a fact, and part is opinion. Which is which?

5. Is Tomi likely to wear her kimono when she is back in the United States? Will she continue flower arranging? Will she hide her feelings? Give reasons for your answer to each question.

_____

_____

_____

_____

_____

_____

SKILL FOCUS

The following questions will help you figure out the theme of "A Simple Arrangement." Thinking about the title and the characters will help you infer the message of the story.

1. Think about the title of the story. To what kind of arrangement does it refer?

_____

_____

2. Who is having difficulty with this arrangement? Why?

_____

_____

3. What Japanese customs are difficult for her?

_____

_____

4. Why is Tomi's visit to her grandparents' garden a turning point for her?

_____

_____

5. What is the author's message or theme? _____

_____

_____

_____

6. How does family love help Tomi and her Japanese relatives reach a happy solution to their conflicts? _____

_____

▶ **Real Life Connections** Describe an experience where you felt—like Tomi did—as though you could do nothing right.

Lesson 12

Cause and Effect

___ Reading a Social Studies Selection

▶ **Background Information**

After World War II, the Allied forces occupied Germany. Tensions between the Soviet Union and the Western Allies forced the division of this country into two. The Communist government built the Berlin Wall, which divided the city of Berlin. It took twenty-eight years for the wall to come down and unite the two countries once again.

Before you read this selection, preview it. Previewing will help you understand the main ideas in the selection. First, look at the title. Then read the headings in boldfaced type. Read the first and last paragraphs; they often give a summary of what is in the selection. Finally, study the pictures and read the captions.

▶ **Skill Focus**

Many events that you read about in your textbooks are connected by **cause and effect**. A cause is a reason, condition, or situation that makes an event happen. An effect is the result of a cause.

Often, several causes will result in one effect. Read the example in the box. As you read, try to understand how

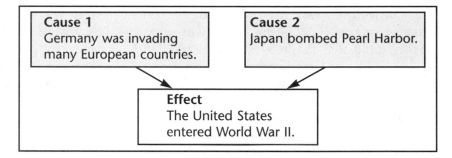

One cause may also have several effects. Read the example below.

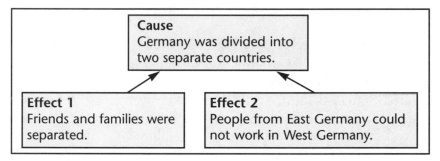

causes and effects are connected.

▶ **Word Clues**

Read the sentences below. Look for context clues that explain the underlined word.

> In return, the Soviets brought their currency to the eastern part of the city and blockaded Berlin. They blocked off all roads, railways, and canals, and turned off power lines that supplied power from East Berlin to the western side of the city.

The word *blockaded* in the first sentence is explained in the next sentence, which gives details that help you understand that something

that is blockaded is blocked or difficult to pass through.

Use **detail** context clues to find the meaning of the four underlined words in the selection.

▶ **Strategy Tip**

As you read the selection, look for cause and effect connections. Many of the events in "The Rise and Fall of the Berlin Wall" had several causes or several effects. Be aware of such cause and effect connections when you read other selections.

The Rise and Fall of the Berlin Wall

For 28 years, the Berlin Wall divided Berlin, once the proud and beautiful capital of Germany. The concrete wall stood nine to twelve feet and zigzagged for 28 miles through the center of the city. Another 70 miles of wall separated all of West Berlin from East Germany. The Berlin Wall was like a deadly moat that made West Berlin an island in the middle of East Germany.

To understand how it happened that a wall was built that kept neighbors, friends, and families from getting together or even seeing one another except maybe from apartment windows that were higher than the wall, it is important to know about the history of Germany and the rest of Europe.

Germany Struggles After World War I

✗ Germany was defeated in World War I in 1918 by the Allied forces, which included the United States, Britain, and France. The war was devastating for Germany. The country lost about two million soldiers, and millions more had been wounded. Under the Treaty of Versailles, Germany was forced to give up much of its territory to the Allies and pay $33 billion in <u>reparations</u> for war damage.

The new German government faced an enormous economic challenge, and it failed. Inflation skyrocketed. At one point, German workers were taking their pay home in wheelbarrows because the German money was nearly worthless. The 1929 depression that spanned the globe hit Germany particularly hard. There were no jobs and little food. Germans were very bitter and believed that they were still being unjustly punished for the war they had lost. People were looking for a leader to solve their problems and make Germany a wealthy country again.

Adolph Hitler, the leader of the National Socialist German Workers Party (also called the Nazi Party), promised Germans that he could make Germany successful again. He said that Communists were trying to destroy Germany, and he blamed Jews for the economic depression. By 1933, he had become the head of the German government.

World War II Changes Germany Forever

Hitler was able to convince many Germans that they were a "super race" of people who deserved to rule the world. After so much bitter frustration, many were ready to take up arms and claim that power. Germany had already taken over Austria and Czechoslovakia before World War II began in 1939, with Hitler's invasion of Poland. Denmark, Norway, Belgium, Luxembourg, and France all fell to Hitler even before Germany and Italy joined forces. In 1941, Germany broke an alliance it had with the Soviet Union and instead attacked that country. Also in 1941, Japan, as an ally of Germany, attacked Pearl Harbor, a U.S. military base in the Pacific Ocean. Afterward, the United States declared war on Japan, and Hitler declared war on the United States.

✗ By the time the war ended in 1945, the devastation and suffering all over Europe were enormous. About 55 million people died. About six million Jews were killed by the Nazis just

An armed soldier patrols the east side of the Berlin Wall to prevent people from escaping to West Berlin.

because they were Jewish. Germany itself lost about six million people. Germany was left to <u>reconstruct</u> itself once again.

✗ This time, the rest of the world was going to have a say in how Germany built its power. The United States, Britain, and the Soviet Union formed the European Advisory Commission and divided Germany into four zones. Each country, including France, was supposed to occupy one zone to be sure that Germany could not build up a military force again. The occupation was supposed to be temporary. The city of Berlin was in the Soviet zone, but because Berlin was the capital of Germany, the countries divided Berlin into four zones of occupation.

The division of Germany wasn't easy, however. The United States, Britain, and France agreed to stop <u>dismantling</u> Germany and to begin to help its economy recover. This made the Soviets angry and relations between the Western countries and the Soviet Union grew more tense. The nations that had been friends in World War II were becoming enemies.

Tensions Grow Between East and West

✗ Meanwhile, the Soviets were committed to spreading Communism, and Western leaders were concerned. In the years that followed, the rivalry between the United States and the Soviet Union grew. In 1948, the Soviets tried to force the Allies to leave Berlin and limited entry to West Berlin, but the Allies refused to leave. France, Britain, and the United States united their three zones into a single zone, and much to the anger of the Soviets, they used West German money in this new zone.

In return, the Soviets brought their money to the eastern part of the city and blockaded Berlin. They blocked off all roads, railways, and canals, and turned off power lines that supplied power from East Berlin to the western side of the city. It is estimated that the people of West Berlin could have survived only six weeks with all 80 entry spots to the city sealed off. Some people thought that all American, British, and French troops would have to leave Berlin to the Soviet Union. Instead, on June 26, 1948, planes came from all over the world to deliver supplies to West Berlin. By the next year, the Soviets turned the electrical power on again.

The Cold War Begins

The Berlin blockade signaled the start of the Cold War. People in the West began to think of Soviets as enemies who would be willing to go to war for the sake of spreading Communism. Germans began to think of the Allied forces more as their protectors than as occupying troops.

The Cold War continued, and East Germany and West Germany officially became separate countries in 1949. The Western countries offered financial assistance to help West Germany get back on its feet, and the economy gradually grew stronger. In East Germany, however, the Soviets were gaining more control and increasingly limiting the freedom of the citizens. Soon, literature, newspapers, theater, art, and radio were only mouthpieces for the government. In addition, the economy was terrible. The Soviet economy was completely controlled by the state and did not create much wealth. Living conditions were poor, food was scarce, and jobs paid very little.

✗ West Berlin was always a problem to the Communists. It sprouted as a prosperous city right in the middle of the poverty of East Germany. East Germans went to Berlin often, and many East Germans even had jobs there. Those who worked in West Berlin were paid much better and could afford to live well. This upset the East German government, but what upset the leaders even more was that many people used West Berlin as an escape route. East Germans would come to the city, and then they would stay there or the West German government would help them to travel to other parts of the West.

As the population in East Germany declined, the people who stayed grew more and more upset at the conditions they faced. In 1953, the dissatisfaction turned into a real uprising in East Berlin's main square. Rioters opened jails and filled the streets in mass demonstrations. The Soviets sent in armed troops, and about 800 East Germans were killed, 240 of them East Berliners. This was the first time that the Soviets used military force to control people in another country, and it further widened the gap between the East and the West.

The Cold War grew worse, and through the 1950s, East Germans continued to flee to the West through Berlin. On August 13, 1961, the East German government made a strong move. Soviet troops ringed Berlin, and 10,000 East German soldiers stood behind them ready to fight. Workmen lined the border between East and West Berlin. They dug in concrete posts that they strung with barbed wire—wire with sharp spikes on it that is used to make fences. Then the workers erected the wall.

✘ The wall that made an island of West Berlin was probably the most guarded wall in all the world. Thirty thousand troops patrolled 193 watchtowers, 208 bunkers, and other watch posts. The guards were ordered to shoot escapees on sight, and shoot they did. Over the 28 years that the wall stood, many people managed to escape over the wall or under the wall in tunnels, but many people were also killed by East German border guards.

Through the 1960s and 1970s, tensions between the Communist and democratic worlds went up and down. With arms control agreements in 1972, the Cold War seemed to be warming up, but the Vietnam conflict and the Soviet invasion of Afghanistan had tensions high again by the end of the 1970s.

Tensions Begin to Ease

The 1980s brought about changes in leadership and changes in the rivalries. Mikhail Gorbachev became the first secretary of the Soviet Communist Party in 1985 and introduced policies of openness and economic restructuring to the Soviet people. Because Eastern European countries took their leads from what the Soviet Union did, East German leaders watched all this nervously, not knowing what it would mean for their country.

✘ What Gorbachev's policies eventually meant for Eastern Europe truly was an opening of possibilities and opportunities for self-government. In 1989, Poland held its first free elections since the 1930s. In mid-1989, Hungary opened its borders with the West. Because East Germans were permitted to travel within Communist-ruled countries, people fled through Hungary and its open borders to Austria and then West Germany, which guaranteed them citizenship.

The East Germans who remained grew more restless as they saw reform come to their neighboring countries. In early November 1989, more than 500,000 people marched in a peaceful demonstration in East Berlin, and other <u>demonstrations</u> went on in other East German cities. The East German government promised changes and tried to keep control. Finally, the government decided that if people were free to go back and forth to West Germany, perhaps they would not feel the need to emigrate, or leave the country.

The Gates Open

✔ On November 9, 1989, the government announced that the border between East and West Germany was finally open. The announcement came in the evening, and by midnight crowds of East Berliners came to the wall to cross by foot, bike, or car into West Germany. West Germans greeted them with applause and cries of joy. After 28 years, the opening of the wall seemed almost incomprehensible! People could go back and forth without any fear of being shot. Even the East German border guards were friendly to the East Germans crossing over.

Celebrations continued over the days and weeks as the wall came down, and the two Germanys got to know one another again. The economic and political situations in

After the Berlin Wall was torn down, people freely entered and left East and West Berlin through large holes that had been cut out of the wall.

the two countries had been so different for so long, that it took much time and debate for the two countries to figure out how to become one again. France, Britain, the United States, and the Soviet Union held talks with the two Germanys. Finally, at midnight on October 3, 1990, East Germany became a part of West Germany, and the two nations were once again one country! Friends and family were reunited in their home country.

RECALLING FACTS

1. What happened after Western Allies introduced West German marks in West Berlin?

_____

_____

2. a. In the 1950s, what was the economy like in East Berlin?

_____

_____

   b. In the 1950s, what was the economy like in West Berlin?

_____

_____

3. Why were Germans searching for a strong leader after World War I?

_____

_____

4. Reread the paragraphs that have **X**'s next to them. Underline the sentence that states the main idea in each paragraph.

5. Circle the correct meaning of the underlined word in each sentence.

   a. If you lose the only copy of my story, you'll have to give me reparations for my loss.

   payments   repairs

   b. The doctor said that she could reconstruct my broken nose.

   rebuild   remove

   c. We have been dismantling the furniture in preparation for our move.

   repair   take apart

   d. To protest the lack of daycare, the working mothers organized several demonstrations at the mayor's office.

   parties   marches

INTERPRETING FACTS

1. Do you think the World War I Allies made a good decision when they insisted that Germany pay so much in war reparations?

_____

_____

2. Why did the Allies occupy Germany after World War II?

_____

_____

_____

3. What would have happened if planes from around the world didn't fly supplies to West Berlin when it was blockaded?

_____

_____

4. Who suffered more from the Berlin Wall, East Berliners or West Berliners?

_____

_____

_____

5. Reread the paragraph with a check mark next to it. Circle the letter next to the sentence below that states its main idea.

   a. People from East Germany and West Germany were thrilled and unbelieving that the border was open.

   b. In fall of 1989, the border between East and West Germany was open.

   c. Border guards were happier than anyone else about the news.

   d. East Germans and West Germans were happy, but could not understand each other very well.

6. Study the two photographs and their captions on pages 40 and 42. Then compare and contrast East Berlin as it was in 1961 and 1989.

   After the wall was built: _____

   _____

   _____

   After the border was opened: _____

   _____

   _____

SKILL FOCUS

Many cause and effect relationships are described in "The Rise and Fall of the Berlin Wall." In some cases, one cause had several effects. In others, one effect had several causes.

A. Two causes are listed below. On the lines provided, write the effects of each cause.

1. Cause   Germany was defeated in World War I.

   Effects   a. _____

             b. _____

2. Cause   Gorbachev introduced policies of openness.

   Effects   a. _____

             b. _____

B. Two effects are listed below. On the lines provided, write the causes of each effect.

1. Causes   a. _____

            b. _____

   Effect   Countries around the world flew supplies into West Berlin.

2. Causes   a. _____

            b. _____

   Effect   Before the end of the Cold War, many East Germans emigrated to the West.

▶ Real Life Connections   Name two effects of something that you did or said today. Then name one or more causes for something that happened today, either at home or at school.

Diagrams

Reading a Science Selection

▶ Background Information

This selection is about the nervous system and how it works in the human body. All of our behavior in daily life depends on our nervous system, from serious thinking and emotional responses to physical reactions, such as moving away from a source of pain.

Preview "The Nervous System" before you read it. Read the headings and words in boldfaced type. Four diagrams explain some of the ideas in the selection. These diagrams will help you understand how the information in the selection is organized. The selection begins with the smallest unit of the nervous system, the neuron, and progresses to the larger units of the nervous system.

▶ Skill Focus

Textbooks often contain **diagrams** to show what is being explained in the paragraphs. Diagrams can be best understood when you read the paragraphs first. At the end of a paragraph, you might see a reference to a diagram, such as *See Figure 1.*

At that point, you should study the diagram.

When you study a diagram, be sure to read the **caption** and the **labels.** The caption is the statement under the diagram that tells the reader what the figure shows. The labels are the words or phrases that identify parts of the diagram. They usually contain important information.

Use the following steps for reading a selection with diagrams.

1. Read the paragraph before each diagram. Then study the diagram and read its labels and caption. The paragraph below the diagram may also explain what is pictured. Read that paragraph, too.
2. Read the rest of the paragraphs. Look back at the diagrams whenever you think they will help you.
3. After you have finished reading the paragraphs and studying the diagrams, look away from the selection. Try to picture what you have read and the details in the diagrams. If you are not able to do this, read the material again.
4. Follow this method until you understand all the ideas in the selection.

▶ Word Clues

Read the sentence below. Look for context clues that explain the underlined word.

> It is divided into two <u>hemispheres,</u> or halves, by a deep groove.

If you do not know the meaning of the word *hemispheres,* the phrase, *or halves,* can help you. The phrase *or halves* is an appositive phrase. An appositive phrase explains a word coming before it and is set off from the word by commas or dashes.

Use **appositive phrases** to find the meaning of the three underlined words in the selection.

▶ Strategy Tip

When you read "The Nervous System," be sure to follow the four steps for reading a selection with diagrams. Many training manuals use diagrams. Learning how to read them can be useful to you on a job.

The Nervous System

The nervous system is the body's communication system. It carries messages about the outside world and about the body itself. It carries messages that allow muscles to move. It also keeps the body's organs functioning.

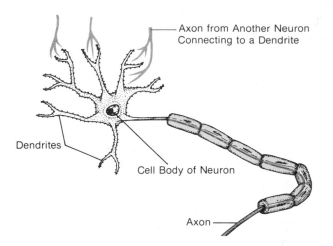

Figure 1. The neuron is the basic unit of the nervous system. Messages are sent by the axon and received by the dendrites.

Neurons

The basic unit of the nervous system is the **neuron** (NOO ron), or nerve cell. A neuron has three parts. It has a cell body and two kinds of threads that extend from it. The long thread is the **axon** (AK son), and the short threads are the **dendrites** (DEN drytz). See Figure 1.

Some neurons have more than one dendrite, but most neurons have only one axon. The dendrites carry messages to the cell body. The axon carries messages away from the cell body. The axon of one neuron connects to the dendrite of another. When a message travels through the nervous system, it is sent by the axon of each neuron. The dendrite receives the message from the axon and passes it on to the next neuron.

Nerves are bundles of neuron fibers, or threads. Different kinds of nerves perform different functions in the nervous system. **Sensory** (SEN sor ee) **nerves** carry messages to the brain and the spinal cord. **Motor nerves** carry messages from the central nervous system to the body's muscles. **Connecting nerves** connect sensory and motor nerves. See Figure 2.

Parts of the Nervous System

The nervous system has two basic parts. The **central nervous system** is made up of the brain and the spinal cord. The **peripheral** (pə RIF ər əl) **nervous system** is made up of the nerves that branch out from the brain and the spinal cord. The **autonomic** (aw toh NOM ik) **nervous system** is a part of the peripheral nervous system. It is made up of the nerves that regulate the internal organs of the body.

Central Nervous System The brain is like the switchboard of a telephone system. Most of the "calls" from the outside world travel through the nerves to the brain. The brain

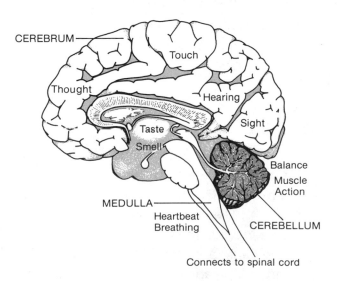

Figure 3. The brain is the center of the nervous system. It has three parts.

Figure 2. Different kinds of nerves perform different functions.

takes in the information from the nerves and sends out orders through the nerves. Although the brain is the principal control center, the spinal cord also plays a major role in receiving and sending messages to the sensory and motor nerves.

The brain itself is divided into three main parts: **cerebrum** (SER ə brəm), **cerebellum** (ser ə BEL əm), and **medulla** (mi DUL ə). See Figure 3. The cerebrum is the largest part of the brain. It is divided into two hemispheres, or halves, by a deep groove. The left hemisphere controls the right side of the body. It is thought to affect the use of language, mathematics, and logical thinking. The right hemisphere controls the left side of the body. Scientists think it affects musical and artistic ability and emotions. Information from the five senses comes to the cerebrum. The cerebrum is the thinking part of the brain. This is where memory is stored. The cerebrum controls all conscious activity, or those activities of which you are aware.

The cerebellum is located underneath the cerebrum. It controls balance and movement of the muscles. The cerebellum also regulates how groups of muscles work together. For example, it <u>coordinates</u> the movements between the hands and the eyes that allow a person to catch a ball—that is, it makes the hands and eyes work well together. The cerebellum affects <u>involuntary</u> activity, the kind of activity of which you are not conscious.

The medulla is the part of the brain that regulates the body's <u>internal</u> organs—the organs inside the body. It controls such vital activities as breathing, the beating of the heart, and the digestion of food. It also controls sneezing, coughing, hiccuping, vomiting, and swallowing.

The medulla connects directly to the spinal cord. The spinal cord is a long bundle of nerves that extends down through the backbone. All messages to or from the brain go through the spinal cord.

Peripheral Nervous System The peripheral nervous system is made up of the nerves that connect the central nervous system to the rest of the body. *Periphery* means "outer edge."

The brain is like the switchboard of a telephone system.

The peripheral nervous system reaches the outer parts of the body, including the hands and feet. See Figure 4.

Nerves of the peripheral nervous system work closely with the central nervous system. The optic nerve, for example, connects the back wall of the eye to the brain. When a person sees something, the eyes receive the image. The image is then sent to the brain by the optic nerve. The brain then "tells" the person what he or she is seeing.

Not all messages are carried to the brain. The nerves can bypass the brain for faster reactions. When a person touches something hot, for example, he or she doesn't first think "hot" before moving. The person moves almost instantly, without thinking. This is called a **reflex action.** In a reflex action, the command to move is sent from the spinal cord instead of the brain.

The autonomic nervous system controls the beating of the heart, the digesting of food, and breathing. *Autonomous* means "independent." The autonomic nervous system works independently of a person's thoughts. The heart beats, food is digested, and breathing continues automatically. The medulla is the

Brain

Spinal Cord

Peripheral Nerves

Peripheral Nerves

Figure 4. The peripheral nervous system reaches the outer parts of the body.

control center for the autonomic nervous system. Messages that begin in the medulla keep the body's internal organs functioning.

The **sympathetic** (sim pə THET ik) and the **parasympathetic** (par ə sim pə THET ik) systems are the two parts of the autonomic nervous system. The sympathetic system works to speed up the heart and send more blood to the muscles during times of physical activity, anger, or stress. The parasympathetic system works to slow down the heartbeat and send blood back to the digestive system during times of rest. In these ways, the body always gets the power and rest that it needs.

RECALLING FACTS

1. What is a neuron?

_____

2. What is the purpose of dendrites?

_____

3. How is the axon different from dendrites?

_____

4. What activities do scientists believe are affected by the left side of the brain?

_____

_____

5. What activities do scientists believe are affected by the right side of the brain?

_____

_____

6. What is the purpose of the autonomic nervous system?

_____

_____

7. Complete each sentence by filling in the correct word.

   involuntary   internal   coordinates

   a. The engine and the transmission are

   among the _____ parts

   of a car.

   b. A social director_____

   activities.

   c. When the pupil of the eye enlarges in

   bright sunlight, it is a(n)

   _____ action.

INTERPRETING FACTS

1. A reflex action is faster than an action that involves thought because the nerve message that causes it
   - || **a.** travels a shorter distance.
   - || **b.** occurs when a person is angry.
   - || **c.** is hotter.

2. Which of the following would cause a reflex action?
   - || **a.** stepping on a sharp rock

   - || **b.** seeing a good friend
   - || **c.** deciding what to order in a restaurant

3. If a person saw a charging lion, which part of the autonomic nervous system would react?
   - || **a.** sympathetic system
   - || **b.** parasympathetic system
   - || **c.** peripheral system

4. When a person awakens from a nap feeling refreshed, it is because the parasympathetic nervous system has

  || **a.** stopped the body's functions.

  || **b.** speeded up the body's functions.

  || **c.** slowed down the body's functions.

5. If the heart did not have nerves,

  || **a.** it would expand.

  || **b.** it could not receive the message to beat.

  || **c.** it would not be part of the central nervous system.

6. If a person is left-handed, which hemisphere of the cerebrum controls the activity of writing?

  || **a.** left

  || **b.** right

  || **c.** both

7. If a person is ambidextrous and can use both hands equally, then the

  || **a.** two hemispheres of the cerebrum can both control writing.

  || **b.** cerebellum is stronger than the cerebrum.

  || **c.** spinal cord is as strong as the brain.

SKILL FOCUS

1. Look at Figure 1. Put a check mark on the cell body. Put a *D* next to a dendrite and an *A* next to the axon.

2. Look at Figure 2. In your own words, explain how the nervous system might work if a person sees danger and runs from it.

_____

_____

_____

_____

3. Look at Figure 3. Name the three parts of the brain and the function of each part.

_____

_____

_____

_____

4. In your own words, explain what is shown in Figure 4.

_____

_____

_____

_____

▶ **Real Life Connections** Which part of the human nervous system are you most interested in studying?

Decimals

Reading a Mathematics Selection

▶ **Background Information**

You probably do not use the word *decimals* often, but you use decimals almost every day of your life.

Decimals are used to measure the amounts of many things that you buy. Packages of meat, fish, and chicken usually show their weight in decimals, for example, "1.5 lbs." That means the package weighs one and a half pounds. Almost every time that you buy gas for your car, the gas meter shows how much gasoline you have bought in decimals, for example, 10.67 gallons. When you buy boxes of breakfast cereal or cake mix, often the label will tell the amounts of different vitamins in the food in decimal amounts. Bottles and boxes of multiple vitamins tell you how much of each kind of vitamin each pill contains.

Every time that you look at a bill or see the price of your purchases on a cash register, you also read decimals—for example, $12.65, $8.34. The decimals in these amounts of money are cents—65 cents and 34 cents. These decimals show you what part of a dollar (100 cents) these amounts are: 65 cents is 65 parts of a dollar; 34 cents is 34 parts of a dollar.

The following selection explains decimals. You will learn the names for the four place values to the right of the decimal point.

▶ **Skill Focus**

Some numbers are written with **decimal points.** A decimal point separates the number into two parts. The digits to the left of the decimal point are whole numbers. The digits to the right of the decimal point are parts of a whole.

126.73

In the number above, 126 is the whole number. The decimal point shows that 73 is part of a whole. When you read this number, you use the word *and* in place of the decimal point. It is read like this: one hundred twenty-six *and* seventy-three hundredths.

As a warm-up for this lesson, see if you can give the answer to the following questions.

If your class has twenty students in it, including yourself, what part of the class are you?

If your club dues are one dollar a week and your allowance is fifteen dollars a week, what part of your allowance are your club dues?

▶ **Word Clues**

The suffix *th* can be added to a number word. When *th* is added to ten, hundred, or thousand, the value of the number word is made less. A *hundred* kilometers is very different from a *hundredth* of a kilometer. If you run a *hundred* kilometers, you have run ten thousand times farther than a *hundredth* of a kilometer. The suffix *th is* used with any place value to the right of the decimal point.

▶ **Strategy Tip**

The suffix *th* is an important clue in reading decimals. It is always used when naming any place value to the right of the decimal point. Failure to use this suffix will confuse people about what number amounts you are using.

READING DECIMALS

Each place to the left of the decimal point shows a value. These are whole numbers.

6 1 , 2 8 4 . 3 9 5 7

The whole number in the number above is sixty-one thousand, two hundred and eighty-four. The members in all the places of this number—61,284—have values of one or more. Places to the right of the decimal point are decimal places. They show values of less than one. The suffix *th* is used in naming each decimal place. The places to the right of the decimal point are tenths, hundredths, thousandths, and ten-thousandths.

6 1 , 2 8 4 . 3 9 5 7

The tenths place is the first place to the right of the decimal point. A number in the tenths place is $\frac{1}{10}$ as large as the same number in the ones place. Think about a dollar bill. It takes 10 dimes to make a dollar. A dime is one-tenth of a dollar. One-tenth can be written as a decimal, 0.1 or as a fraction, $\frac{1}{10}$. A dime is 0.1 or $\frac{1}{10}$ of a dollar.

The hundredths place is the second place to the right of the decimal point. A number in the hundredths place is one-hundredth of the same number in the ones place. It takes 100 pennies to make a dollar. A penny is one-hundredth of a dollar. One-hundredth can be written as a decimal, 0.01, or as a fraction, $\frac{1}{100}$. A penny is 0.01 or $\frac{1}{100}$ of a dollar.

The thousandths place is the third place to the right of the decimal point. A number in the thousandths place is one thousandth of the same number in the ones place. This is a very small part of a dollar, and no coin is made for that value. One-thousandth of a dollar is called a *mil*. Mils are used in the financial world. It takes 1,000 mils to make a dollar. One-thousandth can be written as a decimal, 0.001, or as a fraction, $\frac{1}{1,000}$. A mil is 0.001, or $\frac{1}{1,000}$ of a dollar.

The ten-thousandths place is the fourth place to the right of the decimal point. A number in the ten-thousandths place is a ten-thousandth of the same number in the ones place. This is an even smaller part of a dollar than a mil. One ten-thousandth can be written as a decimal, 0.0001, or as a fraction, $\frac{1}{10,000}$.

A number with digits only in the decimal places can be written in two ways.

0.7 or .7

These two numbers have the same value. You read this number as though it were a whole number: seven. Then you add the name of the place value: tenths. The number is read like this: seven tenths.

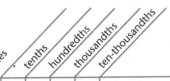

ones	.	tenths	hundredths	thousandths	ten-thousandths	
0	.	7				seven tenths
0	.	0	4			four hundredths
0	.	6	1			sixty-one hundredths
0	.	0	0	2		two thousandths
0	.	8	3	5		eight hundred thirty-five thousandths
0	.	0	3	4	2	three hundred forty-two ten-thousandths
0	.	9	0	3	1	nine thousand thirty-one ten-thousandths

A number that includes digits on both sides of the decimal point is read in two groups.

9,295.17

First, read the digits to the left of the decimal point as a whole number: nine thousand two hundred ninety-five. The decimal point stands for the word *and*. Then read the decimal value as though it were a whole number: seventeen. Then add the name of the place value of the last digit: hundredths. The number is read like this: nine thousand two hundred ninety-five and seventeen hundredths.

The number can also be written as a whole number and a fraction. The decimal number is written as a fraction. The whole number remains the same. Because 7 is in the hundredths place, the denominator of the fraction is 100. It is read the same as the decimal number.

$$9,295\tfrac{17}{100}$$

Read the following number.

263.783

Read the digits to the left of the decimal point first. Then say the word *and* when you reach the decimal point. Read the digits to the right of the decimal point. Because the last digit is in the thousandths place, add the word *thousandths*. The number is read like this: two hundred sixty-three and seven hundred eighty-three thousandths. The number is written as a whole number and a fraction as follows:

$$263\tfrac{783}{1,000}$$

Look at the following number.

49.5036

It is read like this: forty-nine and five thousand thirty-six ten-thousandths.

Remember, the decimal point separates the whole numbers from the numbers that are less than one whole. The numbers to the right of the decimal point are always less than one.

RECALLING FACTS

1. Write the place values for each digit in this number.

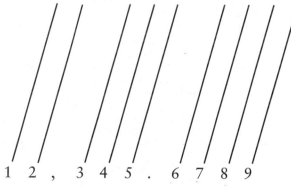

1 2 , 3 4 5 . 6 7 8 9

2. When you hear *and* in a number being read, it means a ——————————.

3. If a dollar bill is one, what part of a dollar is a dime? a penny? a mil? Write each as a fraction and a decimal.

$0.10 = ————— = —————

$0.01 = ————— = —————

mil = ————— = —————

INTERPRETING FACTS

1. Where do you see decimals and fractions used in your daily life?

————————————————

————————————————

2. These numbers all have the same digits. Why do the numbers have different values?
   0.015 .0015 .0105

————————————————

3. Circle the smallest value in each row.
   a. .7   .04   .001
   b. .04   .102   .5
   c. .317   .0146   .09

4. Circle the largest value in each row.
   a. .08   .095   .2
   b. .27   .41   .0896
   c. .1   .275   .09

A. Write each number in the correct column.

	ten thousands	thousands	hundreds	tens	ones	tenths	hundredths	thousandths	ten-thousandths
54 and 9 tenths									
6,702 and 8 tenths									
7 hundredths									
1 and 38 hundredths									
7 thousandths									
91 thousandths									
643 thousandths									
56 and 2 thousandths									
312 and 54 thousandths									
6 ten-thousandths									
923 ten-thousandths									
1,246 ten-thousandths									
172 and 73 ten-thousandths									
4,317 and 6,431 ten-thousandths									
80,008 and 8 ten-thousandths									

B. Write the fraction for each decimal.

0.2 _____   0.0091 _____   884.18 _____

0.65 _____   6.9 _____   329.861 _____

0.634 _____   45.05 _____   25.0106 _____

0.4372 _____   2,379.025 _____   7,563.4007 _____

C. Draw lines to match the decimals and the fractions.

.789	$\frac{789}{1,000}$	789 thousandths
78.9	$78\frac{7,809}{10,000}$	7 and 8,009 ten-thousandths
7.089	$78\frac{9}{10}$	78 and 9 tenths
78.09	$7\frac{89}{1,000}$	78 and 9 hundredths
78.7809	$7\frac{8,009}{10,000}$	78 and 7,809 ten-thousandths
7.8009	$78\frac{9}{100}$	7 and 89 thousandths

▶ **Real Life Connections** Where do you see decimals and fractions used in your daily life?

Vowel–Consonant Combinations

The vowel-consonant combinations *air, ear,* and *are* can stand for the same sound. The words *hair, bear,* and *square* have the same vowel sound, but the letters that stand for the sound are different in each word.

Read the sentences below. Choose a word from the list to complete each sentence. Write the word on the line.

share	**prepare**	**pears**	**stare**
wear	**stairs**	**chair**	**fair**

1. Theo's favorite fruit is ———————.

2. Clarkstown School is having a book ——————— next week.

3. Jorge helped his father ——————— dinner by making the salad.

4. You should never ——————— at the sun without protective glasses, or you will damage your eyes.

5. My sister and I ——————— clothes.

6. It is considered proper to push your ——————— in before you leave the table.

7. Sarah likes to ——————— heavy sweaters in the winter.

8. You have to walk up two flights of ——————— to get to my apartment.

The vowel-consonant combination *ear* can stand for different sounds. The words *bear, earth,* and *beard* have the same vowel letters followed by *r,* but the vowel sound the letters stand for is different in each word.

Read the sentences below. Choose a word from the list to complete each sentence. Write the word on the line.

clear	**search**	**fear**	**early**
heard	**careful**	**learn**	**square**

1. When Warren lost his key, we had to ——————— to find it.

2. Have you ——————— the news about Governor Harris?

3. We got up ——————— every morning when we camped last summer.

4. Elena will ——————— how to drive a car next year.

5. Many people ——————— certain kinds of animals.

6. The sky is always bright blue on a ——————— day.

7. Please be ——————— when you cross the street.

8. A ——————— has four equal sides.

Syllables

Guide 3: Words with a Prefix or Suffix

A prefix always has at least one sounded vowel. This means that a prefix always contains at least one syllable. You can divide a word that has a prefix between the prefix and the root word.

misspell   mis spell

Most suffixes have at least one sounded vowel. This means that a suffix usually contains at least one syllable. You can divide a word that has a suffix between the root word and the suffix.

quickly   quick ly

Divide each of the words below into two syllables between the prefix or suffix and the root word. Write each syllable separately on the line to the right of the word.

1. backward _____
2. worthless _____
3. mistrust _____
4. impure _____
5. fearful _____
6. biplane _____
7. rainy _____
8. midday _____

9. statement _____
10. preheat _____
11. painter _____
12. nonsense _____
13. nearness _____
14. redo _____
15. mistreat _____
16. yearly _____

Guide 4: Words with Two Consonants Between Two Sounded Vowels

A word that has two consonants between two sounded vowels is usually divided into syllables between the two consonants.

winter   win ter

Divide each of the words below into two syllables. Write each syllable separately on the line to the right of the word.

1. signal _____
2. blanket _____
3. master _____
4. admit _____
5. plastic _____
6. sandal _____
7. helmet _____

8. window _____
9. escape _____
10. dentist _____
11. walnut _____
12. napkin _____
13. magnet _____
14. perfume _____

Lesson 17

Prefixes

A **prefix** is a word part that is added to the beginning of a word to change its meaning. Eight prefixes and their meanings are given below.

Prefix	Meaning
bi	having two, or happening every two
de	away from or undo
mid	middle
non	not
semi	half or partly
sub	under or below
tri	having three, or happening every three
uni	having only one
re	again

Read each word below and the meaning that follows it. Write the correct prefix before each word.

1. _____ day   middle of the day
2. _____ monthly   once every two months
3. _____ frost   to become unfrozen
4. _____ freezing   below freezing
5. _____ sweet   partly sweet
6. _____ rail   to go off the rails

7. _____ angle   a shape with three angles
8. _____ circle   half a circle
9. _____ cycle   one-wheel vehicle
10. _____ sense   not making sense
11. _____ play   play again

Use one of the words above to complete each sentence below.

1. It is so cold outside that it must be _____.

2. Another word for twelve o'clock noon is _____.

3. We sat in a _____ around the fire.

4. Mr. Barker had to _____ his refrigerator.

5. A _____ is difficult to ride because it has only one wheel.

6. I read the letter, but it sounded like _____.

7. Broken track caused the train to _____.

8. Our craft club meets _____.

9. The baker used _____ chocolate to make this cake.

10. In geometry class, we learned how to measure the angles of a _____.

11. Because they tied their last game, the two teams had to _____ it.

Stated or Unstated Main Idea

When you read a textbook or reference book for information, the main idea of each paragraph will often be stated in a sentence. The rest of the paragraph will contain the supporting details that give additional information about the main idea.

Sometimes the main idea of a paragraph is not stated in one of the sentences. The information given in the paragraph will help you to **infer**, or figure out, the main idea yourself. To do this, think of a sentence that summarizes the supporting details of the paragraph.

Read the following selection. Decide if the main idea in each paragraph is stated or unstated.

Nō and Kabuki Plays

1. Plays are an important form of entertainment in most countries. Two ki drama unique to Japan are Nō and Kabuki. Music is used in both types of drama. Originally, men performed both men's and women's parts in Nō and Kabuki plays. Bu similarities end there.

2. Kabuki costumes are fancy, bright, and heavy. On the other hand, Nō costumes are quite simple. Kabuki stages are huge and are elaborate. Nō stages are only 18 feet (5.4 meters) square. The only scenery used is a background wall with a tree painted on it. audience must use a lot of imagination.

3. Nō plays started in the 14th century to entertain the upper classes. All parts of a Nō play must follow a certain set of rules. A Nō actor may look as if he is sleepwalking. The action of the play is slow. Certain actions stand for certain things. For example, a few steps forward mean the end of a journey. An important part of a Nō play is the choru chants much of the story.

4. Kabuki plays were developed in the 17th century for the common people. Theate was the main amusement of the merchants of that time. Kabuki plays reflect the merchant's happy moods. The players wear thick makeup and exaggerate their movements and facial expressions to communicate feelings

5. Music is important to Kabuki plays. Kabuki actors sing, dance, and speak their lines to music in the background. Musicians play instruments, such as flutes, drums, and gongs They also use the samisen, a three-stringed instrument shaped somewhat like a banjo. Another common instrument has two small blocks of wood that are banged on the floo

For each paragraph in the selection, if the main idea is stated, write the word *stated* on the line. If the main idea is *unstated,* choose a main idea from the sentences given below and write the letter on the line.

a. Because Kabuki plays are more exciting, they are more popular than Nō plays.

b. A Nō play is noted for its rules and for the controlled movements of the players.

c. Kabuki plays reflect the gaiety and showiness of 17th century Japanese merchants.

d. One difference between Nō and Kabuki plays is that Nō is simpler.

e. Kabuki actors exaggerate their movements to show emotions.

Paragraph 1 _____   *Paragraph 3* _____   *Paragraph 5* _____

Paragraph 2 _____   *Paragraph 4* _____

Go back to each paragraph that has a stated main idea and underline the sentence with the main idea.

Lesson 19

Following Directions

Choking occurs when food or another foreign body completely blocks the air passage, making it impossible to breathe or speak. A person choking on food could die in as little as four minutes. A first-aid technique called **abdominal thrusts** can be used to rescue a choking person. This procedure forces the object blocking the breathing passage out through the mouth.

If a choking victim can either speak or cough, he or she should be encouraged to cough up the object. If the person cannot cough up the object, call an ambulance. If a victim cannot speak or cough, he or she is not getting air, and abdominal thrusts should be used. Choking victims who cannot speak should signal for help by clutching their throat.

Carefully read the information below to learn how to help someone who is choking.

First Aid for the Choking Victim
Abdominal Thrusts

WHAT TO LOOK FOR IN THE VICTIM
1. Cannot speak or breathe
2. Skin turns blue
3. Collapses

Universal sign for choking

WITH THE VICTIM STANDING OR SITTING

1. Stand behind the victim or behind the victim's chair if he or she is sitting. Wrap your arms around the victim's waist.

2. Place the thumb side of your fist against the victim's abdomen, above the navel and below the rib cage.

3. Grab your fist with the other hand and give quick inward and upward thrusts into the abdomen. Repeat these thrusts until the object is forced out or the victim becomes unconscious.

4. If the victim is sitting, stand behind the victim's chair and perform the procedure the same way.
5. After the object is dislodged, the victim should see a doctor for follow-up care.

WHEN THE VICTIM IS UNCONSCIOUS
1. Straddle both of the victim's legs.
2. Place the heel of one hand on the middle of the abdomen just above the navel. Place the other hand on top. Point the fingers of both hands toward the victim's head.
3. Give quick thrusts toward the head and into the abdomen.
4. After giving five thrusts, lift the victim's lower jaw and tongue with your fingers and thumb. Slide one finger down inside the victim's cheek and try to hook the object out.
5. After the object is dislodged, the victim should see a doctor for follow-up care.
NOTE: If you are alone and start to choke, press your abdomen onto a firm object, such as a counter, desk, or table.

A. Below, in incorrect order, are the steps for performing abdominal thrusts when the victim is standing or sitting. Write *1* in front of the step to follow first, *2* in front of the step to follow next, and so on.

_____ Place the thumb side of your fist against the victim's abdomen, above the navel and below the rib cage.

_____ Stand behind the victim or behind the victim's chair if he or she is sitting.

_____ Repeat these thrusts until the object is forced out or the victim becomes unconscious.

_____ Wrap your arms around the victim's waist.

_____ Grab your fist with the other hand and give quick inward and upward thrusts into the abdomen.

B. Read the statements about abdominal thrusts and write *true* or *false* on each line.

_____ 1. A victim is a person who gives first aid.

_____ 2. When food completely blocks the air passage, it is impossible for a person to breathe or speak.

_____ 3. Abdominal thrusts require that the choking victim be slapped on the back four times.

_____ 4. Abdominal thrusts can be done with the victim standing, sitting, or lying on his or her stomach.

_____ 5. Someone choking can perform abdominal thrusts on himself or herself if no help is around.

_____ 6. If a choking victim cannot speak or breathe, he or she is not getting any air.

_____ 7. If a piece of meat blocks a person's air passage, that person will be unaware of it.

_____ 8. Abdominal thrusts force food down a choking person's throat into the stomach.

_____ 9. The rescuer faces the victim who is lying down.

_____ 10. A rescuer may need to repeat abdominal thrusts several times to free the object blocking the air passage.

_____ 11. You could save a person's life using abdominal thrusts.

_____ 12. After abdominal thrusts, the victim should see a doctor for follow-up care.

C. Write the answer to each question. Use complete sentences.

1. For what kind of emergency are abdominal thrusts used? _____

_____

2. Why do you think it is important for everybody to know how to perform abdominal

    thrusts? _____

3. Why are choking victims unable to speak or breathe? _____

_____

4. Rescuers use their hands differently depending on the position of the choking victim.

    What do they do with their hands for standing or sitting victims? _____

    What do they do for victims lying down? _____

5. How should you let someone know that you are choking? _____

_____

6. What is the value of having only one sign to indicate choking? _____

_____

7. What are the three signs that someone is choking on food? _____

_____

8. When would some choking victims be lying down rather than standing or sitting?

_____

Lesson 20 _____

Mood

Reading a Literature Selection _____

▶ **Background Information**

Dolphins are intelligent, air-breathing, warm-blooded sea animals. To sailors the sight of a school of dolphins playing in the ocean means good luck. In this story, a whole town mobilizes to help a school of dolphins whose luck has run out.

▶ **Skill Focus**

Mood is the atmosphere, or feeling, in a story. The mood of a story can be lively, serious, suspenseful, or humorous. An author creates mood by using vivid phrases and details. Sometimes an author repeats a phrase or two to make the mood stronger or more obvious. Setting also influences a story's mood.

Read the paragraph below. Notice the underlined phrases and details that help build a mood of suspense.

The <u>abandoned beach house</u> stood <u>isolated on the dunes</u>. It was <u>too quiet</u> as far as Pat and Chris were concerned. There before them stretched the <u>long, dark, dirty hallway</u>. They knew that they would have to step through it to get to the other room. Slowly, <u>a door creaked open</u> at the back of the house. Pat felt <u>a sudden chill</u>. <u>A small gust of air ruffled Chris's hair</u>. "Who's there?" they called. "Who's there?" they called again. Still <u>no one answered</u>.

Phrases and details like "a door creaked open," "a sudden chill," "a small gust of air ruffled Chris's hair," and "no one answered" help create a mood of suspense. Repetition of the phrase "Who's there?" heightens the suspense. Even the setting—an "abandoned beach house," "isolated on the dunes," and a "long, dark, dirty hallway"—contributes to the mood. The reader does not know the answer to the question "Who's there?"

An author builds a mood of suspense to keep the outcome of a story uncertain. A mood of suspense also helps catch the reader's interest.

▶ **Word Clues**

Read the sentence that follows. Look for context clues that explain the underlined word.

He ran the nylon rope over the <u>winch</u>, which looked like a spool with a crank at the side.

If you don't know the meaning of the word *winch,* the phrase *looked like a spool with a crank at the side* can help you. The appearance of a winch is compared to that of a spool. A phrase that uses the word *like* or *as* to compare two unlike things is called a simile.

Use **comparison** context clues to find the meaning of the three underlined words in the selection.

▶ **Strategy Tip**

As you read, think about the sounds and sights that an author uses to describe the story's setting. Look for vivid phrases and details. What mood has the author created? How does the setting contribute to the story's mood?

The Dolphin Disaster

Skreek—a single sea gull wheeled across the low, gray sky. The fog was closing in on Port Hegen like a dirty cotton curtain. Most of the lobster boats were still outside the harbor. Ralph Hemming was busy setting his lobster traps when he spotted the first of the dolphins.

"Must be two hundred, maybe three hundred dolphins out there," he said, using the radio that linked his boat to shore. "Odd. Haven't seen them this close to shore in years."

Annie Sloan's voice came over the radio. "Had some up at the Cape last year. Paper said that over a dozen died. Got trapped in shallow water."

The radio crackled as another voice came in. "Hey, Ralph. You got Spooner with you?"

Hemming swung his rumbling boat toward a bright red float that marked one of his sunken traps. He pressed the microphone button. "He's on the wharf mending some of our traps."

"Too bad," said the other voice. "Spooner might have an idea why they're headed so close to the shallows. He knows all about these things."

Other voices on the radio agreed. Meanwhile, Ralph Hemming was busy hooking up his trap line, a rope tied to the trap. He ran the nylon rope over the winch, which looked like a spool with a crank at the side. By turning the crank, the winch would pull the heavy wooden trap up from the bottom, a hundred feet below.

Ralph thought about his son, Spooner. For a sixteen year old, Spooner knew the sea well. He was always reading about the sea and its creatures. In some ways, he knew more about the ocean than some adults who had spent their lives on the water. One thing was sure, though. Spooner wouldn't fish for a living like his grandfather and father. Oh, he'd work with the sea all right, but he'd probably pursue his goal of studying ocean science. Spooner <u>aspired</u> to be an oceanographer just as much as many boys his age dreamed about becoming football players.

Dolphins! Hundreds of them arching out of the water in sleek, dark curves!

Spooner was so struck by the sight that he dropped the lobster trap that he was mending. He ran to the end of the wharf.

The dolphins were in the middle of the channel, moving toward Bald Point. Spooner strained his eyes, but the fog, edging nearer to shore, made it difficult to see the dolphins clearly.

Spooner scrambled down the worn wooden steps to the pebbly beach. His shoes clattered on the smooth stones. The tide had already begun to go out. Pushing his family's rowboat to the water's edge, Spooner floated it and jumped in. He swung the small outboard motor into the water and yanked on the rope several times. This will be the day that the motor won't start, he thought. Finally, the motor buzzed into life.

The fog was getting thicker. In a matter of moments, the dolphins would be swallowed up in the thick folds of the fog. Spooner headed the boat out into the channel. He knew the waters of this rocky coast by heart. He knew that he could track down the dolphins.

Even so, Spooner nearly missed them in the fog. The narrow entrance to Bald Point Cove was only fifty feet wide, with low cliffs rising on both sides. Catching a movement in the water out of the corner of his eye, Spooner swung his boat toward land. Beaching the craft, he sprinted up the low cliff on one side of Bald Point Cove.

The little <u>cove</u> was like a soup bowl three hundred yards across. At high tide, the water in the cove was twenty feet at its deepest. At low tide, the cove was a stretch of mud.

Spooner stood looking down at the cove. Below, he saw hundreds of dolphins swimming around the small pool. They darted this way and that, circling, confused. Something was very wrong.

Then Spooner remembered the story in the paper last year. More than twenty dolphins had died in shallow water off Cape Cod. Some scientists believed that the dolphins' built-in "sonar" had failed for some reason.

Spooner watched as the <u>ebbing</u> tide ran out of the cove like water out of a cracked bowl. The dolphins were swimming faster in crazier circles. He had to get help fast. He'd head for home and get his sister Audrey. She wasn't very interested in the sea, but she was a terrific organizer. She'd help!

Only half an hour later, Spooner and Audrey watched Mr. Shell push back his sleeves and lean against his counter. "Look, kids, I'll be glad to help, but I can't leave the store just now. After six, when I close . . ."

"Then it will be too late!" cried Audrey.

Mr. Shell was the third person in the village Audrey and Spooner had approached. They had gotten lots of sympathy but no help. Spooner had the feeling no one really believed that the danger to the dolphins was so serious! Spooner and Audrey ran out of the store and down toward the town wharf.

> How could they get the animals out of danger? Suddenly, Spooner remembered something that he had read.

"Spooner! Audrey! What's up?" They turned to see Paul Sequeira coming up from the docks. He was seventy two, but he still worked his traps every day as he had for more than fifty years.

"It's dolphins, Mr. Sequeira. Hundreds of them. They're trapped in Bald Point Cove, and the tide will be out soon!" Spooner quickly told Mr. Sequeira what he had seen.

"I heard on the radio that they were close to shore," said Mr. Sequeira. "Fog's so thick, everyone's coming in now. We'll round up some help. Come on."

It seemed only minutes later that Spooner, Audrey, Mr. Sequeira, and nine others hurried to the cove. More help was on the way. Mr. Sequeira had radioed the police, too.

Water was running out of the cove like sand from an hourglass. The water was only three feet deep and getting lower every minute. Spooner couldn't help looking back and forth from his watch to the widening stretch of mud in the cove.

Already a few dolphins were stuck in mud. The others swam frantically in the shallow water. In less than an hour, all the water in the cove would be gone.

How could they get the animals out of danger? Suddenly, Spooner remembered something that he had read. "Form a line! We'll move toward them and herd them into the channel!"

The rescuers moved into the water and did as Spooner said. They forced the dolphins toward the narrow channel leading to the sea. Audrey cheered as some of the dolphins slipped out through the opening.

More people came. They herded more and more animals out to the sea. But the dense fog was making it difficult to see. The dolphins still in the cove darted about desperately. They were frantic and frightened.

"Audrey!" called Mr. Sequeira. "Get out to my boat and radio for some nets. Hurry!"

Audrey splashed through the shallow water, climbed the cliff, and slid down the other side. She rowed quickly but cautiously. The fog had almost totally obscured Mr. Sequeira's lobster boat anchored in the channel. Once on board she made contact with Port Hegen. The nets were on their way. But would they reach the cove in time? Audrey hurried back.

There were about seventy dolphins still in the cove when the water ran out completely. The rescuers couldn't bear to watch the stranded animals die in the mud. They used their heavy nets to drag and tug and slide the heavy animals into the channel.

The workers were able to save about half of the remaining dolphins. The rest had been stuck in the mud too long. Already they were dying.

Later, on the wharf, Ralph Hemming put his arms around his son and daughter. "You did your best, kids. That's all you can ever do."

"Aye," said Mr. Sequeira. "If it hadn't been for you kids, hundreds of dolphins would have died. Think of the hundreds that we saved."

Spooner blinked away tears. "I know we saved most of them. But I can't help thinking that if we knew why they swam into the cove, we could have saved all of them."

In spite of the tragedy, Spooner's dad smiled to himself. He could see that his son planned to spend even more time in the library learning about the ocean. Perhaps there was a positive outcome after all.

RECALLING FACTS

1. Who is the main character?

_____

2. Who is Paul Sequeira?

_____

_____

3. How did the dolphins become trapped?

_____

_____

_____

4. Why did Spooner get his sister?

_____

5. List two methods that the rescuers used to save the dolphins.

_____

_____

_____

_____

6. Why did some dolphins die in spite of the rescue efforts?

_____

_____

_____

_____

7. What was the climax, or the most exciting event, of the story?

_____

_____

_____

8. Draw a line to match each word with its meaning.

aspired   small, sheltered body of water

cove   had the ambition to be or do

ebbing   something flowing back, as the tide does toward the sea

INTERPRETING FACTS

1. Circle three character traits that Spooner showed during the rescue.

selfishness   ambition   concern

determination   intelligence   laziness

2. Choose one character trait and tell how Spooner demonstrated that trait during the rescue.

_____

_____

3. What effect did the sighting of dolphins have on the people of Port Hegen?

_____

4. Why do you think that some of the people in Port Hegen were willing to work so hard to save the dolphins?

_____

_____

5. Why was Mr. Hemming proud of Spooner and Audrey?

_____

_____

_____

6. Circle the letter next to the statement that best states the theme of the story.
   a. Living near the sea is dangerous.
   b. Dolphins often get stranded in coves when the tide goes out.
   c. People working together can overcome almost any problem.

Vivid phrases and details along with setting help create mood in this story. In the following questions, you must decide how the author uses setting and details to catch the reader's interest.

1. Several incidents in "The Dolphin Disaster" have outcomes that are uncertain at first. For example, as you read the story, you may have asked yourself the following questions:

   Will Spooner be able to track down the dolphins?

   Will Spooner get enough help?

   Will the nets arrive in time?

   Will the rescuers save the dolphins before the water runs out of the cove?

   As a result of the uncertainty, what kind of mood, or atmosphere, has the author created?

   _____

   _____

   _____

2. In the list below, circle the letter next to the phrases and details that do *not* develop the story's mood.
   a. Skreek—a single sea gull wheeled across the low, gray sky.
   b. so struck by the sight that he dropped the lobster trap that he was mending
   c. only minutes later
   d. motor buzzed into life
   e. fast-ebbing tide
   f. Dolphins! Hundreds of them
   g. darted this way and that, circling, confused
   h. water was running out of the cove like sand from an hourglass
   i. Audrey was a terrific organizer
   j. looking back and forth from his watch to the widening stretch of mud in the cove
   k. in the library learning about the ocean

3. Setting often contributes to a story's mood. In this story, a fog "was closing in on Port Hegen like a dirty cotton curtain" and "in a matter of moments, the dolphins would be swallowed up in the thick folds of the fog." What effect does the fog have on the mood of the story?

   _____

   _____

   _____

   _____

▶ **Real Life Connections** Name an instance where you have worked on a team with family, friends, or classmates.

Lesson 21

Propaganda

Reading a Social Studies Selection

▶ **Background Information**

In 1898, the United States went to war with Spain. One of the main causes of the war was the sinking of the battleship *Maine.* There was never any proof that Spain sank the ship, yet most Americans believed that Spain was responsible.

▶ **Skill Focus**

Propaganda is the spreading of information and ideas in a way meant to make others accept them. Often the information and ideas are misleading. Propaganda usually distorts the truth to convince people to believe or to do something that will further a particular cause.

Propaganda may include many facts, but the facts are usually chosen because they support the writer's point of view. Often only one side of a story is told. The facts are usually presented in an emotional way to sway the reader's opinion and to have an effect or impact on a large number of people.

Propaganda can be very dangerous. It can be used for immoral or hurtful purposes. For this reason, knowing how to recognize propaganda is important.

To recognize propaganda, follow these steps.

1. **Identify the facts.**
   Sort the facts from the opinions. A fact is a statement that is true and can be proven. An opinion is a judgment based on personal beliefs and feelings.
2. **Identify errors of fact.**
   Look for ways that facts have been changed or slanted and information that has been left out to suit the aim of the propaganda.
3. **Analyze the emotional appeal.**
   Decide how the language of the propaganda tries to affect the reader's emotions.
4. **Reach conclusions.**
   Ask what the purpose of the propaganda is and whether this purpose has been achieved.

▶ **Word Clues**

If a reading has no context clues to explain an unknown word or phrase, there may be a clue elsewhere. Read the sentence below.

These newspapers had a great influence on public opinion.[1]

Notice the raised number after the phrase *public opinion.* This number is a signal to you to look for a footnote with the same number at the bottom of the page. A **footnote** gives a brief definition or explanation of the phrase.

[1] public opinion: the expressed views of a group of people about issues of common interest or concern; views not based on what is certain but on what the people as a whole think to be true or likely.

Sometimes the footnote includes a respelling to show you how to pronounce the word.

Use **footnote** context clues to find the meaning of the three other numbered words or phrases in the selection.

▶ **Strategy Tip**

The selection describes the background to the sinking of the *Maine.* It contains two primary sources: a message from Captain Sigsbee and a newspaper report. As you read, notice how propaganda was used to turn the American public against Spain.

Remember the Maine

On February 15, 1898, the United States battleship *Maine* sat in the harbor of Havana, Cuba. Suddenly, the *Maine* blew apart in a huge explosion. Two hundred sixty American sailors were killed.

To this day, no one is sure what caused the explosion. The ship's captain gave no cause for the disaster in his report. A navy investigation failed to uncover any clear evidence. Yet, most Americans believed that Spain blew up the ship. Across America people repeated, "Remember the *Maine.*" Emotions ran high. Soon the American people demanded war with Spain.

Why did Americans think that Spain had sunk the *Maine*? Why were they so eager to go to war? The story of the *Maine* is an important lesson in American history.

Dangers to Peace

In 1898, the United States was at peace. America had fought in no major war since the Civil War. A generation had grown up without knowing the horrors of war. The nation took peace for granted.

✗ But several events were occuring that were dangerous to peace. Some Americans wanted the United States to become a world power. They were called imperialists, or empire builders. They dreamed of an American empire. Some Americans had an extreme pride in America's growing power. They were called jingoists. Jingoists thought that America should show its strength by a warlike policy toward other nations. Another danger to peace came from several of America's leading newspapers. These newspapers tried to sway their readers' emotions to support a war. They paid little attention to facts in their news stories. These newspapers had a great influence on public opinion.[1] They played an important role in the story of the *Maine*.

Cuba

The island of Cuba is ninety miles (144 kilometers) off the southeastern coast of the United States. In the 1890s, it became a focus of American interest. Businesses had invested money in Cuba's sugar fields. Politicians recognized Cuba's geographic and military importance to the United States. Americans in general were concerned about the political situation in Cuba.

For years, Cuba had been under Spanish rule. Many Cubans wanted independence. In 1895, some Cubans attempted a revolt against Spain. The revolt failed. Spain sent a new governor, General Weyler, to the island. He treated the rebels cruelly. He set up detention camps[2] in which many Cuban prisoners became sick and died.

Americans were shocked by the news from Cuba. They wanted to know more about what was happening. Two New York newspapers saw a chance to sell more copies. They made Cuba a hot news topic.

Yellow Journalism

The two New York papers were Joseph Pulitzer's *World* and William Randolph Hearst's *Journal*. These newspapers competed with each other for stories about Cuba. They printed shocking stories with screaming headlines. In these stories, Spain was always the villain. A group of Cubans in New York was feeding information to the papers. Its information was slanted in favor of the rebels.

Yellow journalism is a kind of propaganda.

The stories in the *World* and the *Journal* had little to do with the facts. Instead, they tried to catch the readers' attention and sway their emotions. This kind of journalism became known as yellow journalism. Yellow journalism is a kind of propaganda.

✗ ✗ With great emotion, the newspapers

---

[1] public opinion: the expressed views of a group of people about issues of common interest or concern; views not based on what is certain but on what the people as a whole think to be true or likely.

[2] detention camps (di TEN shən KAMPS): places where people are held temporarily as prisoners. In an attempt to cut off supplies to Cuban rebels, General Weyler ordered peasants to gather in detention camps.

reported about conditions in Cuba. One article read: "You would sicken at the sight of thousands of women and children starving to death in Cuba today . . . filthy skeletons dying on bare, foul boards." Another paper stated in an editorial: "If Spain will not put an end to murder in Cuba, the United States must."

✔ The two newspapers urged the United States to go to war with Spain. Hearst told one photographer who was going to Cuba, "You supply the pictures. I'll supply the war." The stories that the New York papers carried had a great effect. They were picked up by newspapers all over the country. Public opinion became set against Spain.

The Sinking of the *Maine*

Riots erupted in Havana, the capital of Cuba, in 1898. President McKinley ordered the battleship *Maine* into Havana harbor. He wanted to protect American citizens in Cuba. Shortly after the *Maine* arrived in Havana, it exploded.

Captain Sigsbee was the officer in charge of the *Maine*. He immediately made the following report about the explosion.

Maine blown up in Havana Harbor at nine-forty tonight and destroyed. Many wounded and doubtless more killed or drowned. Wounded and others on board Spanish man-of-war[3] and Ward Line steamer. Send lighthouse tenders[4] from Key West for crew and the few pieces of equipment above water. No one has clothing other than that upon him. Public opinion should be suspended until further report. All officers believed to be saved. . . . Many Spanish officers, including representatives of General Blanco, now with me to express sympathy.

The newspapers reported the explosion to the American people in a very different way. On page 68 is the front page of the *World* on February 17, two days after the explosion.

[3] man-of-war: a fighting ship.

[4] tenders: ships that take care of other ships, supplying food, rescuing crew members, and so on.

War Fever

No one was ever able to prove that Spain sank the *Maine*. The explosion may have been an accident. Or Cuban rebels may have secretly caused it to draw America into war with Spain. Whatever the cause, American public opinion was against Spain.

President McKinley tried to keep war from breaking out. He offered a peace plan to Spain. The plan suggested that Cuba become independent. Spain turned down McKinley's plan.

War fever ran high in the United States. The newspapers kept up their stories against Spain. Finally, President McKinley recognized Cuba as an independent country. As a result, Spain declared war on the United States. The next day, Congress declared war on Spain. The Spanish-American War had begun.

RECALLING FACTS

1. For the effect described in the sentence below, circle the letter next to the correct cause.

   The New York newspapers reported shocking stories about Cuba because

   a. they cared about the Cuban people.

   b. they wanted to sell papers.

   c. they owned property in Cuba.

2. Who gave the *Journal* and the *World* information about Cuba?

   _____

   _____

3. Sequence the following events in the order in which they happened.

   _____ General Weyler came to Cuba as governor.

   _____ Congress declared war on Spain.

   _____ Cubans revolted against Spain.

   _____ The *Maine* sank in Havana harbor.

4. Reread the paragraph with an X next to it. Then underline the sentence that best states the paragraph's main idea.

5. Reread the paragraph with two X's next to it. Underline the sentence that best states the paragraph's main idea. Then circle two details that support the main idea of the paragraph.

6. Why did Spain declare war on the United States?

   _____

   _____

   _____

7. Complete each sentence by writing the answer on the line provided.

   detention camps
   man-of-war
   tenders

   a. A ship that fights or is ready to fight is

   a _____.

   b. Many Cubans died from hunger or

   sickness in _____ set up by Spain's General Weyler.

   c. Survivors of the *Maine* were rescued

   by _____.

1. Match the words in the left column with the attitudes in the right column.

    _____ imperialists   **a.** wanted to prove America's strength

    _____ newspapers   **b.** wanted to use America's power to create an empire

    _____ jingoists   **c.** wanted to sell papers by printing war stories

    _____ Americans   **d.** were convinced that Spain had sunk the *Maine*

2. In 1898, the Cuban people were fighting for independence from Spain. A comparison can be drawn between this struggle and what event in American history?

    _____

    _____

3. Identify each of the following statements as fact or opinion. Circle the letter next to each statement that expresses an opinion.

    a. "If Spain will not put an end to the murder in Cuba, the United States must."

    b. The island of Cuba is ninety miles (144 kilometers) off the southeastern coast of the United States.

    c. America should show its strength by being warlike toward other nations.

4. Cuban rebels might have been responsible for sinking the *Maine*. What could have been their reason for doing it?

    _____

    _____

5. Reread the paragraph with a check mark next to it. Write a sentence stating its main idea.

    _____

    _____

SKILL FOCUS

Use Captain Sigsbee's message and the *World*'s front page to answer the questions below.

1. **Identify the facts** (distinguish facts from opinions).

    a. List the facts in Captain Sigsbee's message. _____

    _____

    b. What opinions can you identify in his message? _____

    _____

    c. List the facts in the *World* report. _____

    _____

d. What information in the *World* report is based on opinion? _____

_____

2. **Identify errors of fact.**
   a. What does Captain Sigsbee say in his message about the cause of the explosion?

   _____

   b. What does the *World* suggest that Sigsbee thinks is the cause?

   _____

   c. What does Sigsbee report about the actions of the Spanish after the explosion?

   _____

   d. Does this information appear in the *World*? _____
   e. How does the newspaper describe Captain Sigsbee's attitude toward the Spanish?

   _____

3. **Analyze emotional appeal.**
   a. Does Captain Sigsbee seem interested in turning public opinion against Spain? _____
   b. What effect would the drawing of the explosion in the *World* have on readers? Why?

   _____

   _____

   c. The third headline uses the word *enemy*. What emotional impact does this word have on readers?

   _____

   _____

4. **Reach conclusions.**
   a. What overall message does the *World* report convey? _____

   _____

   b. What emotional effect does the *World* report have on a reader? _____

   _____

   c. Why might the *World* have slanted its report as it did? _____

   _____

   d. What effect do you think the *World* report had on readers' attitudes toward Spain?

   _____

   e. How might the report have influenced the outbreak of the Spanish-American War?

   _____

   _____

   _____

▶ **Real Life Connections** Where could you find an example of yellow journalism?

Cause and Effect

Reading a Science Selection

▶ **Background Information**

In Chilé, the Alacalufe Indians spend more than three-fourths of their lives in boats on the Pacific Ocean. The ocean is their sole source of food. For this reason, their fishing boats are at sea for weeks at a time. Most of each day is spent fishing.

All over the world, people make their living by fishing. This is true especially of people in coastal towns. However, nearly all of these people have other sources of food. For example, they have farms or gardens where they grow vegetables and fruit to eat. They also buy crops brought from other areas.

Three-quarters of the Earth is ocean. Still, only a small portion of the food that humans eat comes from the sea. This fact may be surprising, but as you will see in this selection, this may change in the future.

▶ **Skill Focus**

The **cause** of an event is the reason it happens. The **effect** is the result of the cause. For example, a blizzard can cause the closing of an airport. The cause is the blizzard. The effect is the closing of the airport.

Sometimes an effect can be the cause of another effect. In this way, a chain of causes and effects is formed. Read the following paragraph.

> There was little rain that year. The lack of rain caused most of the crops to die. As a result, the farmer had few crops to sell. He didn't earn enough money to pay his taxes. Finally, he had to sell his farm.

The following diagram shows this chain of causes and effects.

> little rain → most crops died → few crops to sell → not enough money to pay taxes → sell farm

The first arrow shows how the first cause (little rain) results in an effect (most crops died). This effect is also the cause of an effect (few crops to sell), and so on.

▶ **Word Clues**

Read the sentences below. Look for context clues that explain the underlined word.

> There have been many innovations in farming methods, such as crop rotation and the use of chemical fertilizers. These changes have enabled farmers to grow much more food on an acre of land than they used to.

If you do not know the meaning of the word *innovations*, the word *changes* in the next sentence can help you. The words *innovations* and *changes* are synonyms. Innovations are changes, new ways of doing things. A synonym for an unknown word can appear anywhere in the paragraph.

Look for **synonym** context clues to find the meaning of the three underlined words in the selection.

▶ **Strategy Tip**

When you read "Farming the Ocean," look for chains of causes and effects. Remember, an effect can be the cause of another effect. Understanding cause and effect relationships can help you in all aspects of your life.

Farming the Ocean

The Earth's population has been growing at a tremendous rate. Four hundred years ago, there were only a few million people on the Earth. According to the 1995 U.S. Census, there are over 5.73 billion people, and this number is expected to continue to increase rapidly. One cause of the increase is improved medical care.

The world's supply of food has also been growing very quickly. There have been many developments in farming methods, such as crop rotation and the use of chemical fertilizers. Crop rotation is the practice of planting different crops on a particular piece of land each year. These changes have enabled farmers to grow much more food on an acre of land than in the past. Tractors, reapers, and other farm machinery make it possible to harvest large crops before they die in the field. New methods of transportation and refrigeration make it possible to get food from the farm to the table without spoiling. Special housing and vitamins make it possible to produce more and larger cows, pigs, and chickens.

The growth of the world's food supply must keep up with the growth of the world's population, or people will go hungry. Food shortages in India, Africa, and China have resulted in the starvation of millions of people. In these parts of the world, there is not enough food for the people who live there.

One method that could increase the world's supply of food is called **aquaculture** (AK wə kul chər). Aquaculture is the farming of the oceans. Agriculture is the science and art of farming the land; that is, the <u>cultivation</u> of land to produce crops. The areas of the earth that are covered with water are the <u>marine</u> areas. Aquaculture, then, is the cultivation of the marine areas of the Earth.

People have always used the oceans as a source of food. They have eaten seaweed. They have also gathered and eaten shellfish, such as clams, oysters, and lobsters. They have used spears, hooks, and nets to catch fish. However, none of these traditional methods is aquaculture. These methods take things out of the sea. They do not put anything back into it. Today scientists are thinking about how to care for the oceans and their valuable resources. With special care, the oceans could provide new food supplies.

Agriculturists have learned how to care for the land. They put back in the soil minerals that plants remove. They build shelters for farm animals. They provide all the requirements needed to make their crops and animals healthy. This care has increased the amount of food that the land can produce. The increased production provides food for more people. The same process can work for the oceans.

Aquaculture actually began about three hundred years ago. A Japanese lord was forced to move from one island to another. When he arrived at his new home, he discovered that oysters, his favorite food, were not to be found in the nearby bay. The lord sent his

> *The world's population is growing. Can our world's food supply keep up?*

The ocean continues to be an important source of food.

assistants back to the old island to bring oysters to Japan. Hundreds of oysters were transplanted into the bay. The lord believed that since the oysters lived in one body of water, they could live in another. He was right. The oysters survived in the bay. They produced many young oysters, called **larvae** (LAR vee).

Soon starfish and other predators, like the bat ray, began to eat the oysters. More of the oysters were being eaten by other fish than by people. The Japanese lord had fences built out of bamboo. The long bamboo shoots were stuck into the sand under the water. The other ends of the bamboo reached above the bay's surface. The fences stopped the starfish from crawling into the oyster beds and kept the bat rays from swimming into them.

As the Japanese lord enjoyed his oysters, word of the oyster gardens spread throughout Japan. Other people tried to grow oysters for themselves. Some were successful, but many were not. After many attempts at growing oysters, the Japanese fisher-farmers began to learn from both their successes and their failures. They learned that the oysters needed many things in order to survive. If all of these conditions were not present, the oysters would die. What were some of the requirements for the oysters?

First, it was discovered that water that was too cold would kill the oysters. Then it was found that if the water was too warm, the oysters would also die. The oysters could not survive in lakes or lagoons where the water was not changed by the tides. Moving waters provided the oysters with an unending supply of food called **plankton** (PLANGK tən). Plankton are tiny plants and animals that float in the world's oceans. However, areas with too strong a current would tear the oysters from where they had <u>moored</u> themselves and wash them out to sea. It was also discovered that the

This fish farm in Greece is typical of the aquacultural methods being used in marine areas throughout the world.

oysters would stick to tiles hung in the water. In this position, they got more plankton and thus grew faster and larger.

Before too long, people all over Japan were farming the oceans. Oysters were just one of their underwater crops. They also cultivated, or helped the natural growth of, clams, shrimp, scallops, yellowfish (a kind of free-swimming fish), and many other sea animals.

In more recent times, fish farms have become more numerous in other parts of the world. These farms successfully raise fish, such as salmon, that lay large eggs. The large eggs are easily gathered and moved to protected areas where the newly hatched fish can grow.

Scientists have found that sea animals other than fish can be harvested in tremendous volume. One example is a type of tiny shrimp called **krill**. Krill live in huge swarms in all the world's oceans. They can be processed into a very nutritious food for farm animals. The krill that live in the Antarctic Ocean can be eaten by people.

Today, scientists called marine biologists are observing life in the oceans, seas, and bays all over the world. They are experimenting to improve the methods of aquaculture begun by the Japanese lord three hundred years ago. Many people believe that farming the ocean is the only hope for winning the race between the growth of the world's population and the growth of the world's food supply.

1. Why is it necessary for the world's food supply to keep growing?

   _____

   _____

2. What is aquaculture?

   _____

   _____

3. What are some of the foods people have always taken from the sea?

   _____

   _____

4. Where did aquaculture begin?

   _____

5. What is plankton?

   _____

   _____

6. What are krill?

   _____

   _____

7. Answer each question by writing *yes* or *no* on the line provided.

   a. Is food produced by the cultivation of land? _____

   b. Are seaweeds marine plants? _____

   c. Can a tent be moored by safety pins?

   _____

INTERPRETING FACTS

For the following questions, underline the correct answers.

1. More food gets from the farm to the table without spoiling because of
   a. home refrigerators.
   b. restaurant refrigerators.
   c. refrigerated trucks.

2. Fishing probably provides food mostly in countries that
   a. have large farms.
   b. have coastlines.
   c. have high mountains.

3. One reason aquaculture may have started in Japan is that Japan
   a. is a small country.
   b. is surrounded by the sea.
   c. is a hot country.

4. Crop rotation produces greater yield because
   a. different crops are used for different purposes.
   b. different crops grow at different rates.
   c. different crops use up different minerals in the soil.

For the following questions, circle the correct answers.

1. What is one cause of the increase in world population?
   a. the spread of diseases
   b. better medical care
   c. lower birthrates

2. What are two causes of the increase in the world's food supply?
   a. crop rotation and chemical fertilizers
   b. more farmland and crop rotation
   c. chemical fertilizers and more farm land

3. What is one effect of new transportation methods and refrigeration?
   a. food gets from the farm to the table without spoiling
   b. improved farm machinery
   c. lower crop production

4. Which one of the following would *not* cause oysters to die?
   a. sea water that was too cold
   b. plankton that was too thick
   c. sea water that was too warm

5. According to the article, aquaculture is
   a. a cause of world population growth
   b. an effect of world population growth
   c. neither a cause nor an effect of population growth

6. Three chains of causes and effects can be made from the events listed below. Connect one event from each column with arrows to show the chains. You will not use all the events. You can use some of the events more than once.

a. Minerals are replaced in soil	Bamboo fences are built	Oysters rot	Fewer people go hungry
b. Japanese lord's oysters eaten by predators	More farm animals survive	More food is produced	More oysters are produced
c. Crops become diseased	More storms occur	Predators are kept out of oyster beds	Weeds grow faster
d. Shelters are built for farm animals	Land produces more crops	Fewer storms occur	Less water is available for crops

▶ **Real Life Connections** Do you think that marine biologists should continue to do research on newer and better methods of aquaculture? Tell why or why not.

Word Problems

— Reading a Mathematics Selection —

▶ **Background Information**

A word problem is any practical problem that you need to use math to solve. For example, let's say that one of your parents gives you $10 to go to the movies. You need a ticket, but you also want a small popcorn and a small soda. You ask yourself, "Do I have enough money for all these things?" This question is a word problem.

You can set up the facts of the real-life problem as a math problem in this way: A ticket to the movie costs $6. A small popcorn costs $2.50. A small soda costs $1.50. If Raymond's parents give him $10, will he have enough to buy what he wants?

Add up the numbers. You will see the total cost is exactly $10. The answer is yes.

Knowing how to put the facts of a practical problem into the form of a math problem in this way will help you solve problems that you deal with every day.

▶ **Skill Focus**

To solve the problems in this selection, you will need to do two mathematical operations.

Use the following five steps in solving word problems.

1. Read the problem. Be sure that you are familiar with all the words, especially the labels. Think about the question that is being asked. Try to picture in your mind the information that is given. Read the problem again to be sure that you understand the question.

2. Decide how to find the answer. It may be helpful to write a sentence about each fact that is given in the problem. Is extra information given that is not necessary to solve the problem? After you determine which information, if any, is not needed, decide what operation to use to solve the problem. In solving some problems, you will need to do two operations. If so, you will need to write two mathematical sentences to find the answer. Be sure to look for key words.

3. Estimate the answer. Use rounded numbers to make an estimate for each mathematical sentence.

4. Carry out the plan. Solve each of the mathematical sentences.

5. Reread the problem. Then write the complete

answer. Is the answer logical? How close is it to your estimate?

▶ **Word Clues**

As you read word problems, look for key words that will help you find the answer. In problems in which two operations are needed, you must look for key words for both operations. Words, such as *twice as much* and *all together,* often show that you have to combine many groups of the same size, or multiply. Words like *divided, average,* and *per,* often show that you have to break down one big group into smaller groups, or divide.

▶ **Strategy Tip**

After you read each problem, decide if you have more information than you need to answer the question. If you do, you may find it helpful to cross out the extra information. Then use the five steps with the necessary information to solve the problem.

Solving Word Problems That Have Unnecessary Information

Many facts have been collected about the sea. These facts can be put together to answer new questions about the sea.

Use the following five steps in solving word problems.
1. Read the problem.
2. Decide how to find the answer.
3. Estimate the answer.
4. Carry out the plan.
5. Reread the problem.

READ THE PROBLEM

The *Bathysphere* dove to a depth of 914 meters in 1934. In 1948, the *Benthoscope* dove $1\frac{1}{2}$ times deeper. In 1960, the *Trieste* dove 8 times deeper than the *Benthoscope*. How many meters deep did the *Trieste* dive?

Read the problem again. Be sure that you know the label that is used with each number fact. Are there any words that you do not know? If so, look them up to find their meanings. What question does the problem ask? Often the question is asked in the last sentence. *How many meters deep did the* Trieste *dive?*

DECIDE HOW TO FIND THE ANSWER

The problem gives you many number facts. Written as sentences, the facts are as follows:
1. The *Bathysphere* dove 914 meters.
2. The *Bathysphere* dove in 1934.
3. The *Benthoscope* dove $1\frac{1}{2}$ times deeper.
4. The *Benthoscope* dove in 1948.
5. The *Trieste* dove 8 times deeper than the *Benthoscope*.
6. The *Trieste* dove in 1960.

Enough facts are given in the problem to solve it. However, more information is given than is needed. When extra information is given, decide which facts are not needed and cross them out. In this problem, facts 2, 4, and 6 are not necessary to answer the question.

You will need to do two arithmetic operations to find the answer. You need to find out first how deep the *Benthoscope* dove and then how deep the *Trieste* dove. For the first operation, you must multiply. The key words are $1\frac{1}{2}$ *times deeper*. This is your mathematical sentence:

$$914 \times 1\frac{1}{2} = n$$

For the second operation, you must multiply again. The key words 8 *times deeper* tell you to multiply. This is your mathematical sentence:

$$n \times 8 = m$$

In this mathematical sentence, the letter n stands for the answer to the first operation. The letter m stands for the number of meters the *Trieste* dove.

ESTIMATE THE ANSWER

Use rounded numbers to help make an estimate. Round to the nearest one or hundred.

First operation: $900 \times 2 = n$
$1,800 = n$

Second operation: $1,800 \times 8 = m$
$14,400 = m$

Your estimate is 14,400.

CARRY OUT THE PLAN

Do the arithmetic.

First operation: $914 \times 1\frac{1}{2} = n$
$1,371 = n$

Second operation: $1,371 \times 8 = m$
$10,968 = m$

REREAD THE PROBLEM

After rereading the problem, write the complete answer. The *Trieste* dove 10,968 meters. How close is your answer to your estimate? If your answer is not close, you should start over.

Use the five steps to solve this problem.
Read: In 1930, William Dow extracted 90 micrograms of gold from 12,000 liters of sea water. In 1965, Dr. Bayer extracted 1.4 micrograms of gold from 100 liters of sea water. Who extracted more gold per liter of water?

Decide: The problem lists four number facts.

1. Dow extracted gold in 1930.
2. Dow extracted 90 micrograms of gold from 12,000 liters of water.
3. Bayer extracted gold in 1965.
4. Bayer extracted 1.4 micrograms of gold from 100 liters of water.

The question can be answered using facts 2 and 4. Facts 1 and 3 are not necessary.

You will need to do two arithmetic operations to find the answer. You need to find out first how much gold per liter Dow extracted and then how much gold per liter Bayer extracted. For both operations, you must divide. The key word is *per*. These are your mathematical sentences.

$$90 \div 12{,}000 = d$$
$$1.4 \div 100 = b$$

Estimate: Round each number.

$$100 \div 12{,}000 = d$$
$$.008 = d$$
$$1 \div 100 = b$$
$$.01 = b$$

Carry Out: $90 \div 12{,}000 = d$
$$.0075 = d$$
$$1.4 \div 100 = b$$
$$.014 = b$$

Reread: Bayer extracted more gold per liter of water than Dow.

RECALLING FACTS

1. In which step do you figure out which information isn't needed?

2. How do you make an estimate?

3. What should you do if you have extra information in a problem?

4. Match each operation to its key word.

    multiply   **a.** times

    divide   **b.** per

INTERPRETING FACTS

1. Why might a word problem have extra information?

2. Why are labels important in word problems?

3. In the second problem in the selection, why are the letters *b* and *d* used?

4. Why was the letter *n* used in the first problem and not the second?

_____

_____

To solve these word problems, you will use one or both of only two mathematical operations: multiplication and division. You may find it helpful to write a sentence on another sheet of paper for each number fact that is given. Some problems have extra information. Cross out the facts that are not needed.

1. Read: In 1950, the United States used 757 billion liters of water. Fifteen years later, in 1965, 1.7 times as much water was used as in 1950. Forty-four years later, in 1994, 2.4 times as much water was used as in 1965. How much water was used in 1994?

Decide: _____

_____

Estimate: _____

Carry Out: _____

Reread: _____

2. Read: A seaweed farm that covers 10 square kilometers produces 72,576 metric tons of seaweed. A dredging site that covers 21 square kilometers produces 272 metric tons of gold for a profit of $150 million. Is there more seaweed or more gold in a square kilometer of sea water?

Decide: _____

_____

Estimate: _____

Carry Out: _____

Reread: _____

3. Read: At sea level the air pressure is 1.033 kilograms per square centimeter. This is called *1 atmosphere*. The pressure increases by 1 atmosphere every 10 meters of water depth. At what depth would you find 4 atmospheres of pressure, and how great is the pressure?

Decide: _____

Estimate: _____

Carry Out: _____

Reread: _____

_____

▶ **Real Life Connections** Describe an everyday problem or situation that you would solve using two mathematical operations.

Syllables

Guide 5: Words with One Consonant Between Two Sounded Vowels

Many words have only one consonant between two sounded vowels. This guide will help you in dividing such words. Such words are divided differently depending on whether the first vowel is long or short.

> **Guide 5a:** A word that has one consonant between two sounded vowels, with the first vowel long, is usually divided into syllables before the consonant.

spider   spi der

Use Guide 5a to divide each word below into two syllables by writing each syllable separately on the line to the right of the word.

1. pilot _____
2. robot _____
3. music _____
4. private _____
5. even _____
6. human _____
7. spiral _____
8. minus _____

9. bacon _____
10. odor _____
11. flavor _____
12. major _____
13. locate _____
14. total _____
15. moment _____
16. student _____

> **Guide 5b:** A word that has one consonant between two sounded vowels, with the first vowel short, is usually divided into syllables after the consonant.

rapid   rap id

Use Guide 5b to divide each word below into two syllables by writing each syllable separately on the line to the right of the word.

1. shiver _____
2. robin _____
3. closet _____
4. dragon _____
5. clever _____
6. medal _____
7. travel _____
8. river _____

9. pedal _____
10. magic _____
11. seven _____
12. planet _____
13. second _____
14. melon _____
15. robin _____
16. shovel _____

Say each of the words below to yourself. If the first vowel is long, use Guide 5a
to divide the word into two syllables. If the first vowel is short, use Guide 5b.

1. cabin _____
2. paper _____
3. lilac _____
4. lemon _____
5. silent _____
6. lizard _____
7. meter _____

8. model _____
9. wagon _____
10. clover _____
11. petal _____
12. spinal _____
13. satin _____
14. tiger _____

Guide 6: Words with Blends

The word *zebra* has two consonants between two sounded vowels. Because
the consonant blend *br* makes one sound, it is treated in the same way that
a single consonant is treated. The word is divided in this way: *ze bra*.

In a word that has three consonants between two vowels, it is possible that
two of the consonants are a blend or a digraph. You treat the blend or
digraph as one consonant. For example, *congress* has a *gr* blend. You divide
the word between the consonant and the consonant blend: *con gress*.

Circle the blend or digraph in each of the words below. Then divide the word into
two syllables by writing each syllable separately on the line to the right of the word.

1. explore _____
2. leather _____
3. athlete _____
4. other _____
5. pumpkin _____
6. detract _____
7. camphor _____

8. bushel _____
9. surprise _____
10. gather _____
11. central _____
12. compress _____
13. imply _____
14. children _____

When a word ends in *-le*, the *-le* and the consonant before it make up a
syllable, as in *bun dle*.

Divide the words below into two syllables by writing each syllable separately on
the line to the right of the word.

1. cradle _____
2. gentle _____
3. bugle _____
4. handle _____
5. sample _____
6. stable _____
7. thimble _____

8. fable _____
9. dimple _____
10. noble _____
11. rifle _____
12. title _____
13. maple _____
14. uncle _____

Accented Syllables

When words contain two syllables, one of the syllables is stressed, or accented, more than the other. In dictionaries, the **accent mark** (') is placed at the end of the syllable that is said with more stress. For example, the first syllable in the word *picnic* is said with more stress than the second syllable.

pic'nic

Words that have three syllables usually are accented on one of the first two syllables. When you are trying to pronounce a word with three syllables, say the word with more stress on the first syllable. If the word does not sound right, say it again, giving the most stress to the second syllable.

Say each of the following words to yourself. Write an accent mark after the syllable that should be stressed.

1. peo ple
2. riv er
3. con tain
4. chem i cal
5. pos si ble
6. fig ure
7. con so nant

8. di rec tion
9. hu man
10. im por tant
11. gar den
12. de vel op
13. or gan ize
14. por cu pine

15. car na tion
16. mo tel
17. buf fa lo
18. ca noe
19. wag on
20. tor pe do
21. for get ting

Words of four or more syllables usually have two accented syllables. In the word *caterpillar*, the first syllable, *cat*, has the most stress. This syllable receives the primary accent mark ('). The third syllable, *pil*, has more stress than the remaining two syllables, but less stress than the first syllable. The secondary accent mark (') is placed after that syllable.

cat'er pil'lar

Say each of the following words to yourself. Write the primary accent mark ' after the syllable that has the most stress. Write the secondary accent mark ' after the syllable that has the second most stress.

1. sec re tar y
2. bron to sau rus
3. ar ma dil lo
4. hip po pot a mus
5. cem e ter y

6. e lec tro mag net
7. al li ga tor
8. mar i o nette
9. in vi ta tion
10. en cy clo pe di a

Lesson 26

Schwa Sound

The vowels *a, e, i, o,* and *u* can all have the same sound. This is a soft sound like a short *u* pronounced lightly.

Pronounce *around.* Did the *a* sound like a soft, short *u?* _____

Pronounce *harden.* Did the *e* sound like a soft, short *u?* _____

Pronounce *animal.* Did the *i* sound like a soft, short *u?* _____

Pronounce *collect.* Did the *o* sound like a soft, short *u?* _____

Pronounce *circus.* Did the *u* sound like a soft, short *u?* _____

This short, soft *u* sound is called the **schwa** sound. In dictionary respellings, the symbol ə stands for the schwa sound. If you look up the word *lament* in the dictionary, you will find it respelled this way.

lə ment'

Say each of the words below to yourself. Write an accent mark after the syllable that is stressed. Then circle the letter that stands for the schwa sound.

1. wag on
2. a ware
3. gal lop
4. eas i ly
5. ap ply
6. gar ment
7. pos si ble
8. sup ply
9. ze bra
10. op po site
11. ap pear
12. mov a ble
13. ash en
14. at tack
15. se rum
16. stan za
17. choc o late
18. sug ar
19. mir ror
20. med i cine

Look at the words in the list above. Does the *schwa* sound come in the accented or unaccented syllable? Write the correct word in the sentence below.

The *schwa* sound always falls in an _____ syllable of a word.

Read the selection that follows. Circle the letter or letters in each underlined word that stand for the schwa sound.

Animals in Africa

Africa has many large animals. One of the largest of all beasts is the elephant. It lives in a family herd of blood relatives and travels about eating grass and leaves. The gorilla is another fairly big animal. It is the largest of the apes. It looks fierce, but it is really a peaceful animal.

The lion and the leopard are among the fiercest of the land beasts. The crocodile, which lives in lakes, rivers, and marshes, is much feared. The hyena is disliked because of its horrible shrieks.

Lesson 27

Main Idea and Supporting Details

When you are reading a paragraph that is packed with information, the first step is to find the **main idea**. The second step is to find the **supporting details** that give more information about the main idea. These details are important because they help develop, or support, the main idea.

The following paragraph is about the American colonists. The main idea and supporting details are listed after the paragraph.

> The American colonists were unhappy under the rule of England. In 1774, colonial leaders formed the First Continental Congress to decide on possible actions to take. They asked the King of England to cancel certain laws that the colonists thought unfair. They also asked that British troops leave the colonies.

Main Idea The American colonists were unhappy under the rule of England.

Supporting Details
a. They formed the First Continental Congress to decide on possible actions to take.
b. They asked the King of England to do away with laws that the colonists thought unfair.
c. They asked that the British troops leave.

On the next page, write the sentence that states the main idea for each paragraph. Then write the supporting details in your own words.

1. Both the British and the colonial armies wanted control of two hills near Boston—Bunker Hill and Breed's Hill. In June, 1775, the Americans took control of them first and posted armed troops on Breed's Hill. After two unsuccessful attempts to take the hills, the British defeated the Americans in a battle known as the Battle of Bunker Hill. However, most of the battle was fought on Breed's Hill, not Bunker Hill.

2. In 1776, a new congress, the Second Continental Congress, decided to end British rule and govern the colonies itself. It formed an army to fight the British and made George Washington commander-in-chief. It issued and borrowed money. It set up a postal system and created a navy.

3. The idea of independence spread throughout the colonies. *Common Sense*, written by Thomas Paine, convinced the colonists that they must fight. The colonists in Massachusetts, New Jersey, and South Carolina rebelled against their British governors. A committee set to work on a statement telling the King of England why the colonies believed that

they must break away from England. Thomas Jefferson, with suggestions from the committee, wrote this statement, the Declaration of Independence.

4. A young Frenchman named Lafayette offered to help the colonial army. Later, France declared war on Great Britain. In 1780, France sent 6,000 soldiers to the colonies. The British kept them in Newport Harbor for eleven months. The following spring, the French sent a large squadron of ships and a lot of money. The French had come to the aid of the colonists.

5. In 1781, the colonists won the battle at Yorktown. The British General Cornwallis had marched his soldiers to Yorktown, Virginia. Knowing of Cornwallis's movements, the colonists put into action a plan that ended the Revolutionary War in their favor. Washington and his French allies pretended to move to New York, but marched to Yorktown instead. Meanwhile, the French fleet took control of the waters off Yorktown so that Cornwallis could not get help from the British fleet. Surrounded by these forces, Cornwallis had no choice but to surrender.

Paragraph 1

Main Idea _____

_____

Supporting Details

    a. _____

    b. _____

    c. _____

    d. _____

Paragraph 2

Main Idea _____

_____

Supporting Details

    a. _____

    b. _____

    c. _____

Paragraph 3

Main Idea _____

_____

Supporting Details

    a. _____

    b. _____

    c. _____

Paragraph 4

Main Idea _____

_____

Supporting Details

    a. _____

    b. _____

    c. _____

    d. _____

Paragraph 5

Main Idea _____

_____

Supporting Details

    a. _____

    b. _____

    c. _____

    d. _____

Inferences

In order to understand what an author has not stated, you must gather clues from the details that are stated. In this way, you can **infer**, or figure out, information that is not stated directly in a selection.

If you go through the following steps, you will find it easier to infer information.

1. Read carefully.

2. Think about what you've read. Be sure that you understand the information that is stated.

3. Read again and look for clues to information that is not stated.

4. Put together the information stated with the information that you already know. Use clues to help you make inferences.

As you read the following selection on Phillis Wheatley, pay close attention to the facts. Use the facts to infer information that is not directly stated in the selection.

Phillis Wheatley

1. The year was 1761. Mrs. Wheatley walked out of her large house on an upper-class Boston street. The wife of a successful tailor, she was headed for a slave ship that had docked in the Boston harbor. Although the Wheatleys had a few elderly slaves in their household, Mrs. Wheatley needed a slave who would serve as her personal maid for years to come.

2. Mrs. Wheatley boarded the slave ship. She found hundreds of people cramped in small, dark, stuffy rooms. As she looked around, she was drawn to a thin, frightened-looking girl in a corner. The girl had been kidnapped from her home in West Africa to be sold in America. The long journey had been difficult for her. Mrs. Wheatley paid a small amount for this sickly girl. The ship's captain was pleased because he was afraid that the girl looked too sick to sell at all.

3. The sad life of the young girl was about to undergo a complete change. She couldn't have been bought by a finer master and mistress. The girl reminded Mrs. Wheatley of a tiny tree in need of warmth, food, and care. Mrs. Wheatley named her Phillis, which means "a green branch of a tree." Although the girl spoke only the language of her West African tribe, Mrs. Wheatley explained to her the meaning of her new name. Phillis was pleased with it.

4. Phillis learned quickly. Although she was a servant in the Wheatley home, she was treated more like a member of the family. Instead of doing hard chores, Phillis learned to read English and Latin. She hungrily studied the Bible, mythology, ancient history, and eighteenth-century English poetry. Gradually, Phillis became a well-read woman.

5. Phillis started to write poetry as a teenager. Her first poem, written in 1767, was about the death of George Whitefield, a famous English evangelist. When it was published three years later, Phillis became the first black woman and only the second woman to publish in the colonies. Soon all of Boston knew of her. Her fame spread to England and the rest of Europe as well.

6. Phillis became ill in the early 1770s, and the Wheatleys' family doctor recommended a change in climate. So Phillis accompanied Mr. Wheatley on a business trip to England. She met the best of British society and was well received. With the help of her English friends, her book *Poems on Various Subjects, Religious and Moral* was published.

7. George Washington became commander in chief of the Revolutionary army in 1775. Phillis was delighted that the colonists finally had a strong leader in the fight against England. To express how she felt, Phillis wrote a poem about Washington. She sent it to him with a letter. Much to Phillis's surprise, George

Washington sent her a thank-you note praising her for her beautiful verses and inviting her to visit him. Phillis accepted his invitation.

8. After Mr. and Mrs. Wheatley died, Phillis was left alone. She married John Peters, a freed slave like herself. But he was never able to support the family. Phillis tried to raise money by publishing a second book. She put an advertisement in the newspaper seeking buyers for her book. Much to her disappointment, almost no one showed interest in her work. Shortly thereafter, at the age of 31, she died. Despite all of her hardships, Phillis Wheatley earned great fame as a poet in her time.

For each of the following statements, decide which items can be inferred from the paragraph listed. Put a check mark next to the statement or statements. On the lines that follow, write the phrase or sentence that has the clue that you found. Then explain how you inferred the information.

Paragraph 1 (check two)

a. _____ The Wheatleys were wealthy.

b. _____ The Wheatleys had several children.

c. _____ Mrs. Wheatley was looking for a young maid.

Clue: _____

Explanation:_____

Clue:_____

Explanation:_____

Paragraph 2 (check two)

a. _____ Many of the slaves died on the trip to America.

b. _____ The slave ship carried its passengers as if they were cargo.

c. _____ The healthy-looking slaves brought higher prices.

Clue: _____

Explanation:_____

Clue:_____

Explanation:_____

Paragraph 3 (check two)

a. _____ Phillis was not very good at doing household chores.

b. _____ Phillis had an excellent mind and was eager to learn.

c. _____ The Wheatleys allowed Phillis to read many books in their home.

Clue:_____

Explanation:_____

Clue_____

Explanation:_____

Suffixes

A suffix is a word part that is added to the end of a word to change its meaning. Eight suffixes and their meanings are given below.

Suffix	Meaning	Suffix	Meaning
ity	condition or quality	ous	having, full of
let	small, little	ship	condition of or state of
ly	like or every	ure	act or result
or	person or thing that	ward	toward

Read each word below and the meaning that follows it. Write the correct suffix after each word.

1. mother _____ like a mother
2. back _____ toward the back
3. acid _____ condition of being acidic
4. courage _____ having courage
5. direct _____ person who directs
6. book _____ little book

7. fail _____ act of failing
8. week _____ every week
9. friend _____ state of being friends
10. invent _____ person who invents
11. west _____ toward the west
12. partner _____ state of being partners

Use one of the words above to complete each sentence below.

1. Karen looked _____ to see if she had dropped anything.

2. Tabitha Babbit, the _____ of the circular saw, got the idea for it while watching her spinning wheel.

3. Because a _____ is little, it often has a paper cover.

4. The _____ between Joe and Ben started in second grade.

5. Jumping into the water to save a frightened child is a _____ act.

6. The author was discouraged by his _____ to write a successful novel.

7. The drink's _____ made it taste bitter.

8. Every Friday, Pete bought a _____ supply of groceries.

9. The _____ watched the play from backstage.

10. On Monday, the employees had their _____ meeting.

11. Bill and Pat formed a _____ in order to buy a toy business.

12. The wind was blowing in a _____ direction.

Lesson 30

Library Catalog

To locate a book in the library quickly and easily, use the **library catalog**. In most cases, the catalog will be a computer database. Although formats may vary, most library databases are set up to give the same basic information. You find information by choosing items from a menu, or list. The main menu often lists other resources as well as the library catalog. When you choose the catalog, a second menu will appear. You can then search for a book by its title, by the author's name, or by its subject. If you don't have exact information about the book, you may be able to choose an item called **keywords**. The computer will search its database using one or two important words that you give it.

A library catalog gives more information than just the author, title, and subject of a book. Usually an entry for a book gives a summary, a description (size, number of pages, kind of illustrations), the publisher and date it was published, and a list of related subjects. It may tell how many copies exist, which branches have the book, and whether it is available.

Subject Search

Suppose you want to read a true story about survival in the wilderness. First, you select "Subject" from the catalog menu to do a **subject search.** Then enter a phrase such as *wilderness survival*. A list of subjects will appear. Choose one that is the same as, or close to, the phrase that you entered. A list of books about that topic will appear. Then choose a particular book to find out more about it.

Author Search

If you want to find out which books by a particular author are in the library, you can do an **author search**. Choose "Author" from the catalog menu and enter the author's name, last name first (for example: Ansell, Rod). A list of authors will appear. Choose your author to see a list of his or her books. You can then choose a particular book to find out more about it.

Title Search

If you already know what book you want, you can do a **title search.** Choose "Title" from the catalog menu and enter the exact title. An alphabetical list of titles will appear, including the one that you entered. If the title begins with *A*, *An*, or *The*, the book will be listed by the second word in the title. You can then select the title of the book that you want.

In each kind of search, the last step is to select a particular book. When you do, a screen similar to this one appears:

```
Call Number  Young Adult Nonfiction  Status:
             613.69 An82T                checked
                                         out

AUTHOR: ANSELL, ROD
TITLE: To fight the wild
PUBLISHER: New York: Harcourt Brace
           Jovanovich, c. 1986

DESCRIPTION: 151 p.; ill.; 22cm.
SUMMARY: A man struggles to survive on his
         own in one of the most isolated
         corners of Australia for two months
         before he is rescued.

SUBJECTS: 1) Wilderness areas - Australia
          2) Wilderness Survival
          3) Survival
          4) Australia
```

Notice the call number at the top of the screen on page 90. This number appears on the spine, or narrow back edge, of the book. Every nonfiction book has its own call number that tells where it is shelved in the library. Nonfiction books are kept in numerical order. This book would come before a book with the number 613.7 and after one numbered 612.06. The letters immediately following the number are the first two letters of the author's last name. Across from the call number is the word *status*, which means condition or position. This tells you whether the book is on the shelf or is checked out.

A. Now use the screen on page 90 to do the following:

1. Circle the year that the book was published.

2. Is this book illustrated? Put two lines under the information that tells you.

3. If you wanted to learn more about the setting of this story, what other subjects might you search under? Draw a box around each.

B. Circle the kind of search that you would do in order to answer each question.

1. Who wrote the book *Cowboy: An Album*?

   author search   title search   subject search

2. Which of Virginia Hamilton's books does the library have?

   author search   title search   subject search

3. Does the library have any new books about World War II?

   author search   title search   subject search

4. What is the call number for *The Forgotten Heroes: The Story of the Buffalo Soldiers*?

   author search   title search   subject search

5. Does the library have books on martial arts?

   author search   title search   subject search

6. Does the library have Laurence Yep's newest book?

   author search   title search   subject search

C. Use the information on the computer screen below to answer each question.

1. When was this book published?

   _____

2. The summary mentions a polar expedition. Under what subjects could you look for more information about it?

   _____

   _____

3. Suppose you want to find other books by this author. What name would you look

   under? _____

4. Would this book be shelved before or after one with call number

   J919.804 FAR? _____

```
Call Number  Children's Nonfiction   Status:
         J919.8 DOLAN              checked in

AUTHOR: DOLAN, EDWARD F., 1924-
TITLE: Great mysteries of the ice and snow
PUBLISHER: New York: Dodd, Mead, c. 1985

DESCRIPTION: 117 p.; ill.; 22 cm.
SUMMARY: Discusses unusual creatures and
         events that have been seen or taken
         place in cold climates, including
         sightings of the mysterious Yeti and
         the discovery of the remains of a
         nineteenth-century polar expedition.

SUBJECTS: 1) Curiosities and wonders
          2) Arctic regions - Discovery and
             exploration
          3) Northwest Passage
```

Outlining

Sometimes you write a summary of a selection or a chapter in a textbook to help you understand or study it. Another good way to understand and remember something that you read is to make an **outline** of it. An outline can be written quickly and read easily. A good outline shows how the main ideas and supporting details in a selection are organized.

In a paragraph, the most important idea is the main idea. In an outline of a selection or chapter, the main idea of each paragraph is restated in a few words and written next to a Roman numeral: I, II, III, and so on.

The details that give important supporting information about the main idea are the major details. The major details are written next to capital letters: A, B, C, and so on. These letters are indented, or moved a little to the right, underneath the Roman numerals.

The details that give information about the major details are the minor details. The minor details are written next to numbers: 1, 2, 3, 4, and so on. These numbers are indented underneath the capital letters.

Read the following paragraph. Then look at the outline next to it.

Cargo ships can be classified into different groups according to the kinds of cargo they carry. *General cargo ships* carry packaged items—goods that are put in packages. These include such items as chemicals, food, and furniture. *Tankers* carry liquid cargo. This might include petroleum—the thick natural oil that fuel oil and gasoline are made from—or molasses. *Dry bulk carriers* haul products, such as iron ore and coal, that can be loaded loose on the vessels.

Cargo Ships

I. Classification of cargo ships
  A. General cargo ships
    1. Carry packaged items
    2. Examples—chemicals, food, furniture
  B. Tankers
    1. Carry liquid cargo
    2. Examples—petroleum, molasses
  C. Dry bulk carriers
    1. Carry loose items
    2. Examples—coal, iron ore

Notice that *Classification of cargo ships*, the main idea of the paragraph, is written next to Roman numeral I. *General cargo ships* is written next to capital letter A. This phrase is the first major detail about cargo ships. *Carry packaged items* is written next to number 1. This phrase is a minor detail about general cargo ships.

Every outline should have a title. When you outline a selection, always include at least two main ideas. An outline of a selection can never have a I without a II. There should also be at least two major details under each main idea. An A should always be followed by a B. Finally, there should always be at least two minor details under each major detail.

Each of the following paragraphs compares a type of cargo ship of the past with a type that is in use today. By completing the outline, you will organize information in a way that will help you understand and remember the main ideas and details.

During the early 1900s, the standard general cargo ship was a three-island ship. The first island, called the forecastle, held the crew's quarters. The bridge, from which the ship was navigated, formed the second island in the middle of the ship. The poop, which held the officers' cabins, formed the third island. Today, freighters have one island for the bridge and living quarters. Having one island leaves room for more and bigger hatches and makes it easier to load and unload cargo.

In 1866, the first oceangoing tanker, the *Gluckauf*, was launched. This ship was built in Great Britain for a German oil company. It was 300 feet (91 meters) long and 37 feet (11 meters) wide. It carried 2,300 tons (2,090 metric tons) of oil and could travel at a speed of 9 knots. Large tankers are often called supertankers today. The largest tankers carry about 555,000 deadweight tons. They can travel at a speed of about 15 knots (15 sea-miles per hour).

The first dry bulk carriers were specially designed boats that began hauling iron ore on the Great Lakes during the 1800s. Like tankers, these vessels were designed to carry only one kind of cargo. But unlike tankers, the ore carriers hauled solid cargo. As a result, they required more complicated loading and unloading arrangements than tankers, which needed little more than hose connections and pumps. Today oceangoing bulk carriers have grown larger and larger. Most can carry more than 100,000 short tons (91,000 metric tons) of cargo. Motor-driven equipment on board quickly removes the enormous hatch covers so that the cargo can be reached easily.

II. General cargo ships

    A. Early 1900s—three islands

_____

_____

_____

    B. Today—one island

Reading Drug Labels

Medicine can be helpful in curing an illness but dangerous if taken incorrectly. It is very important to read the label on the bottle or box *before* taking any medication. The label states the medical problems that the medication may help. It gives the dosage—how much medicine should be taken and how often. A label may also provide certain warnings to help prevent the wrong use of the medicine. Anyone using medication should read the label carefully to be familiar with the proper dosage and use.

Read the labels below from two different medications.

FORMULA D—
For coughs due to colds and flu
—quiets coughs
—relieves stuffy nose
—soothes sore throat

DIRECTIONS FOR USE
ADULT DOSE
12 years and over—2 teaspoonfuls
CHILD DOSE
6 to 12 years—1 teaspoonful
2 to 6 years—$\frac{1}{2}$ teaspoonful

Repeat every 4 hours as needed
No more than 6 doses daily
Drink a full glass of water with each dose

WARNINGS
Do not administer to children under 2 years old unless directed by physician. Persons with a high fever or persistent cough or with high blood pressure, diabetes, or heart disease should not use this medication unless directed by physician.

KEEP OUT OF REACH OF CHILDREN

DRAMADON *is the most widely prescribed product for the prevention and treatment of seasickness—including nausea, dizziness, or vomiting.*

DIRECTIONS FOR USE: To prevent motion sickness, take first dose $\frac{1}{2}$ to 1 hour before boarding a ship, boat, plane, car, or bus.

Dosage: Adults: 1 to 2 tablets every 4 to 6 hours, not to exceed 8 tablets in 24 hours. Children 6 to 12 years: 1 tablet every 6 to 8 hours, not to exceed 3 tablets in 24 hours. Children 2 to 6 years: $\frac{1}{2}$ tablet every 6 to 8 hours, not to exceed $1\frac{1}{2}$ tablets in 24 hours.

Warnings: **DRAMADON** may cause drowsiness. Do not operate automobiles or dangerous machinery while taking this medication. Avoid alcoholic beverages while taking this medication. Not for use in the presence of asthma or glaucoma. Keep this and all medication out of reach of children.

A. Use the information on the labels to complete each sentence.

1. The medication used to prevent seasickness is _____.

2. The medication used to quiet coughs is _____.

3. You can tell that Formula D is not a tablet because the directions tell how many _____ to take.

4. Each container of Dramadon contains _____ tablets.

5. The symptoms—or signs—of seasickness are _____.

6. To prevent seasickness from occurring, you should take Dramadon _____ _____.

7. Adults can take _____ Dramadon tablets every 4 to 6 hours. If an adult takes 2 tablets every 4 hours, then _____ tablets will be taken within one day. However, not more than _____ tablets should be taken in a day. This means you can take up to two tablets at one time, but no more than _____ two-tablet doses in a 24-hour period.

8. The Dramadon label warns against driving an automobile while using the medication because the medication may cause _____.

9. If an adult uses the maximum number of Dramadon tablets recommended for one day, then a container of Dramadon will last for _____ days.

10. The medication that should be taken with a glass of water is _____.

11. If an eleven-year-old takes the maximum number of recommended doses of Formula D in one day, then he or she will take _____ teaspoonfuls of the medication. If a four-year-old takes the maximum number of doses in a day, he or she will take _____ teaspoonfuls.

12. If a one-year-old is given Formula D, then a _____ has recommended it.

13. "No more than 6 doses daily" means no more than 6 doses in _____ _____.

B. Circle the letter in front of the one, two, or three answer(s) to each question.

1. Which warning(s) is (are) given on both medications?
   a. Keep out of reach of children.
   b. Do not drive an automobile while using medication.
   c. Do not use if you have glaucoma.

2. Both medications have different dosages for which age group(s)?
   a. children two to six years old   b. children six to twelve years old   c. adults

3. How many teaspoonfuls of Formula D can an adult take every four hours?
   a. 1   b. 8   c. 2

4. What is the most Formula D an adult should take in one day?
   a. 2 teaspoonfuls   b. 12 teaspoonfuls   c. 8 teaspoonfuls

5. What are the benefits of Formula D Cough Syrup?
   a. It helps to relieve a cough.   b. It clears a stuffy nose.   c. It makes a sore throat feel better.

Lesson 33 _____

Setting

Reading a Literature Selection _____

▶ **Background Information**

Today many people know about the sport of mountain climbing. Climbers today make use of the most modern tools and equipment. However, the early mountain climbers were not so lucky. They were pioneers, preparing the way for others in this dangerous sport.

The following selection is a true story about Edward Whymper, the first person to climb the Matterhorn. One of the steepest mountains in the European Alps, the Matterhorn is a challenge to even the most experienced mountain climbers. As you will find out, this great triumph for Whymper ended in tragedy.

▶ **Skill Focus**

Setting is the place and time of the events in a story. Events can happen in any place and at any time. A story can take place on the streets of a city, on a country farm, along a seacoast, or in a foreign country. The time can be the present, several years ago, or far in the future.

In many stories, the setting creates difficulties for the characters. In a story set in a deserted cabin, a person might have to cope with loneliness. In a story set on a ship in a stormy sea, the crew might have to deal with physical danger.

The following questions will help you identify setting and understand how setting can cause difficulties for characters. Ask yourself the following questions as you read a story.

1. Where and when do the events of the story take place?
2. What details does the author use to reveal the setting?
3. What difficulties does the setting create for the characters?
4. How do the characters overcome the difficulties that arise because of the setting?
5. What effect does the setting have on the characters in the story?

▶ **Word Clues**

Read the sentence below. Look for context clues that explain the underlined word.

Young Edward Whymper grew up in England among rolling hills, fertile farmlands, and craggy <u>moors</u>.

If you do not know the meaning of the word *moors*, the words *hills and farmlands* can help you. The word *moors* is grouped with other things in the same category, so that you can figure out that moors are a landform.

Use **groupings** as context clues to find the meaning of the three underlined words in the selection.

▶ **Strategy Tip**

As you read, look for details that describe the setting. Notice how the place and time of the events in this true story cause difficulties for Whymper, the members of his party, and other climbers.

Triumph and Tragedy

Young Edward Whymper grew up in England among rolling hills, fertile farmlands, and craggy moors. He had never seen a mountain or even climbed a hill. That is, not until he came to the Alps at the age of twenty. These fabled mountains stretch through several European countries, including France, Italy, Switzerland, and Austria. Whymper was an engraver who was assigned by a publishing company to make pictures of tall mountains. Since there are no large mountains in England, he came across the English Channel and journeyed over land to see the mountains for himself. And see them he did! These towering snowcapped peaks were like nothing in England. Out of green valleys and clear lakes, the majestic mountains seemed to reach for the sky.

It was 1860, and mountaineering was just becoming known as a sport. A hundred years earlier, Horace Bénédict de Saussure, a scientist from Geneva, offered a reward to whomever could climb the highest peak of the Alps. This peak was Mont Blanc, at 15,771 feet. Six years later, physician Michel Gabriel Paccard and his guide, Jacques Balmat, succeeded. Before Mont Blanc was conquered, mountain climbing was almost unheard of. By the middle of the nineteenth century, however, at least a hundred large peaks in the Alps, such as Ortles, the

Jungfrau, and the Zugspitze, had been climbed for the first time.

The possibilities for conquering <u>sheer</u> peaks for the first time seemed limitless to the earliest mountaineers. However, the surge of interest in climbing prompted one concerned climber to ask sadly in 1854, "Will our grandsons succeed in the future in conquering the last of all the alpine peaks?" The "Golden Age" of alpinism, the climbing of the Alps, had begun. So many English climbers came to explore the peaks of Europe that the Alps became known as the "Playground of Europe." In the two decades that followed, nearly all the important peaks had been conquered.

As difficult as it may be to believe today, the earliest alpine hikers didn't realize that climbing was dangerous, because they had no experience that alerted them to the particular dangers of the sport. It was the ascent and alarming descent of the dramatic Matterhorn that brought about an understanding of the dangers of mountaineering. That is where Edward Whymper returns to the story.

Located on the Swiss-Italian border, the Matterhorn looks like a sharp, pointed pyramid when viewed from the nearby town of Zermatt, Switzerland. Its steep face challenges even the most experienced climbers today.

After journeying in the Alps for almost a year, Whymper first saw the Matterhorn in the summer of 1861. Though he had never climbed a hill before coming to the Alps, he had become interested in climbing during his year in the mountains, and he immediately attempted to climb it. His first attempt failed. Whymper was inexperienced, and the equipment he had was not good enough for climbing such a steep mountain. Even the best mountaineers said that the Matterhorn was impossible to climb. That did not stop Whymper. He resolved to succeed in his climb someday. He spoke of the mountain in the battle terms that many mountaineers use. His plan was "to return with a companion and besiege [or attack] the mountain for so long that either it or we will be beaten."

Whymper thought he had found his companion in Jean Carrel. Carrel grew up in Italy at the foot of the Matterhorn. It had been his dream since he was a young boy to be the first person to climb it. Back in 1857, he had tried to climb it with his brother and another mountaineer, Abbé Aimé Gorret, but the mountain proved overwhelming to the trio. Still, Carrel had every intention of returning to the mountain again, and he knew in his heart that he would succeed.

The two determined men could surely make it together. Whymper went back to England, where he devoted his time to planning for the trip. He created a mountaineer's tent that could be carried.

After an avalanche buried three climbers in 1896 near Vienna, Austria, the first mountain rescue service was founded.

By using it, the climbers could bivouac—make a camp—with some protection from the wind, snow, ice, and cold. A bivouac allows climbers to spend nights on steep rock faces when getting to a flat space would take more than one day. Whymper built new kinds of equipment, such as a <u>grappling</u> iron that could help the climbers grab onto the impossibly steep rock faces. He also built two ladders that could be folded up, which the climbers could carry with them.

In 1863, Whymper was ready. He and Carrel had decided their best route up would be the Italian ridge, but they had to wait for conditions that were suitable for climbing. Certainly there is snow on these high peaks all year round, but the height of summer in a good year is the best chance for success. Finally, in the summer of 1865, all signs indicated that it was time! When Whymper arrived in Italy, he got in touch with Carrel. He found out that his would-be companion had decided to go up with some Italian climbers. What had been a partnership had turned into a rivalry.

Whymper was disappointed but not beaten. He had come this far. There was no way he would turn back now. He found other companions and used his special equipment and newfound expertise to scale the mountain. As it turned out, he and Carrel reached the top on the same day, July 14. Carrel's party was 300 feet below Whymper and his party on the Italian side, so Whymper is considered to be the first person to climb the mountain. Finally, he had realized his dream! The young engraver who had never until five years earlier rested his eyes on a mountain peak had climbed a mountain most people said was impossible to climb.

According to one account by Whymper, his triumphant cries and those of his fellow climbers were heard by Carrel and his party on the Italian side of the peak. Whymper said that he and another climber sent rocks sliding down the mountain to be sure that the Italians knew of their victory. An exultant Whymper said, "The Italians turned and fled."

It didn't take long for Whymper's great joy to turn to grave <u>catastrophe</u>. On the way down the mountain, one of the men in his party slipped. Three of his companions who were attached to the same rope were pulled off the mountain with him. When the rope snapped and the four men fell from the mountain, Whymper could only watch in horror. Afterward, he described the accident: "For a few seconds we watched our unfortunate companions tumble down the slope, fighting with outstretched hands for some kind of finger-hold. They were still unhurt as one by one they disappeared from view and crashed from cliff to cliff down a drop of almost 4,000 feet."

No one knows whether the rope broke in midair or whether it was cut as it slid against a rock. Some people have even suggested that some member of the party cut the rope or gave the climbers who fell a weaker rope. Historians do not believe these theories and point out that until this time, climbers weren't really aware of just how dangerous the sport could be.

Although there had been other deaths and accidents, this disaster quickly changed the way that people thought about mountain climbing. People all over the world heard about the accident. Climbers and nonclimbers began to realize how truly dangerous the pursuit of mountain peaks can be. The more people climbed mountains, the more accidents happened. People can die from slipping off footholds, from pieces of mountain breaking off the main rock face, from exposure to the wind and cold, and from equipment failures. Accidents in which people are injured but not killed make the trip much more dangerous for those in the party who have to carry the injured person. Climbing down a sheer rock wall is already a life-risking course of action.

Trying to do it while carrying a badly hurt climber might be called suicidal.

In 1896, near Vienna, Austria, three climbers were buried by an avalanche. After this, the first mountain rescue service was founded. The service responds to climbers all over the world, and its members have been called "The Angels of the Mountains." Today's climbers wear up-to-date safety equipment and generally train and practice before attempting to climb great peaks. Lightweight but warm clothes, shoes with spikes, and belts that help hold hikers to the mountain are just some of the modern inventions that now help climbers. In addition, climbing clubs and schools around the world teach people proper safety techniques. In the United States, there are even indoor climbing clubs, where people can practice climbing with the safety of soft mattresses to cushion their falls.

Of course, climbing remains dangerous. Avalanches, snowstorms, equipment failures, and carelessness have led to injuries and deaths, but the sport has come a long way since Whymper's climb of triumph and tragedy.

RECALLING FACTS

1. Who was Edward Whymper?

_____

_____

_____

2. Who was his rival from Italy?

_____

3. Why was Whymper's first attempt at the Matterhorn unsuccessful?

_____

_____

_____

4. Why did Whymper need years of preparation before he was ready to return to the Matterhorn?

_____

_____

5. What kind of equipment did Whymper build that he hoped would help him in his climb?

_____

_____

_____

_____

6. What did Whymper and his party do when they reached the top of the Matterhorn?

_____

_____

_____

_____

7. Circle the word that best describes the mood or atmosphere in this story.

adventurous   terrifying   peaceful

Lesson 33 *Identifying setting* **99**

8. Answer each question by writing *yes* or *no* on the line provided.

a. Would a beginning skier learn to ski on a mountain's sheer slopes?

_____

b. Would a sailor use a grappling tool to anchor his boat to another boat?

_____

c. Would a wonderful birthday party be a catastrophe? _____

INTERPRETING FACTS

1. Why do you think Whymper thought that Carrel was his rival?

_____

_____

_____

2. Why might mountain climbers tie ropes around themselves that attach them to one another?

_____

_____

_____

3. How do you think Whymper felt when he returned from the mountain?

_____

_____

_____

4. Whymper had resolved "to return with a companion and besiege the mountain for so long that either it or we will be beaten." Which happened?

_____

_____

_____

5. Circle three traits of character demonstrated by Edward Whymper in his climb of the Matterhorn.

determination	laziness	shyness
inventiveness	resolve	fearfulness

6. a. Using the illustration on page 97, describe in one sentence the clothing climbers wore in the mid-nineteenth century.

_____

_____

_____

b. Using details from the story, how do you think modern climbers would be dressed?

_____

_____

_____

7. Do you think that Edward Whymper would have likely climbed the Matterhorn again?

_____

_____

_____

S KILL FOCUS

Use information in the story and the photographs on pages 97 and 98 to answer the following questions.

1. Where and when does Edward Whymper's climb take place?

_____

2. **a.** Using details from the story, describe the setting in one sentence.

_____

_____

   b. Using details from the photographs, describe the setting in one sentence.

_____

_____

3. What difficulties did the setting create for Whymper and his party?

_____

_____

4. How did Whymper prepare for the setting?

_____

_____

5. What effect did the setting have on Whymper and his party?

_____

_____

▶ Real Life Connections Have you ever engaged in a sport or activity and later realized its dangers? What was your reaction to your earlier behavior?

Reading a Map

Reading a Social Studies Selection

► Background Information

The highest landforms on earth are mountains. By definition, a mountain rises at least 1,000 feet (300 meters) above the land that surrounds it.

At the top of a mountain, the air is thinner than it is at sea level. The thinner air makes it more difficult for people to breathe. Very high mountaintops are covered by snow year round and have very little plant life. This is because mountains are above the **treeline**—the point at which trees can no longer grow.

In many parts of the world, great mountains rise together in groups called ranges. Do you know which mountain range is closest to where you live? It may be one of the eight mountain ranges that are discussed in "The Great Mountain Ranges of the World."

► Skill Focus

A **relief map** shows the differences in height of various parts of the earth's surface, called *landforms.* Some landforms, such as mountains, rise high into the air. Between mountains are landforms called valleys. Other landforms, such as plains, are low and level.

The height of a landform is its **elevation.** Elevation is measured in feet or meters above sea level. Sea level is the point from which the height of all landforms is measured, beginning at zero feet or meters.

Relief maps use colors to show the different elevations and depths of the earth's landforms. Each relief map has a key that is color-coded. This key indicates, in feet or meters, the elevations that the colors on the map stand for.

Another way to compare the height of landforms is to use an illustration drawn with a scale of elevation. This sort of illustration makes it possible to compare landforms that are not close together geographically. The elevation illustration has a **vertical elevation scale.** At the bottom of the scale is sea level. Landforms, such as mountains, are drawn to their proper height according to the elevation scale.

Use both relief maps and elevation illustrations to help you better understand the earth's landforms.

► Word Clues

Read the sentences below. Look for context clues that explain the underlined word.

The Rockies were formed millions of years ago when there was a great underlined{upheaval} in the earth's crust. Hot, liquid rock inside the earth pushed the crust upward thousands of feet above sea level, forming the Rockies.

The word *upheaval* in the first sentence is explained in the sentence that follows it. This sentence gives details that help you to understand the meaning of the word *upheaval.*

Use **detail** context clues to find the meaning of the three underlined words in the selection.

► Strategy Tip

Before you read "The Great Mountain Ranges of the World," preview it. First read the boldfaced headings. Then study the relief map on page 105. Also look at the illustration on page 103. Do you know the elevation of your hometown?

The Great Mountain Ranges of the World

During the long history of the Earth, the mighty forces of nature have been tirelessly at work. These natural forces have shaped the landscape of our world. Among nature's greatest works of art are mountains. Eight major mountain ranges crown the continents of the earth. To the people who live among them, these mountains are things of both beauty and danger.

The Rocky Mountains

The largest mountain range in North America is the Rocky Mountains. This range stretches for more than 3,000 miles (4,800 kilometers) from Canada's Yukon Territory to New Mexico. In places, the Rockies are 350 miles (560 kilometers) wide. The highest peak is Mount Elbert in Colorado. It rises 14,433 feet (4,399 meters) above sea level.

The Rockies were formed millions of years ago when there was a great upheaval in the earth's crust. Hot, liquid rock inside the earth pushed the crust upward thousands of feet above sea level, forming the Rockies. Glaciers, wind, and rain have, over time, carved them into a variety of shapes and sizes. The Rockies form a huge, high wall. For this reason, they are called the Continental Divide. On one side of the Divide, rivers flow east toward the Gulf of Mexico and the Atlantic Ocean. On the other side, rivers flow west toward the Pacific.

The Rockies were an obstacle for settlers in the East who wanted to move to the West. When the South Pass was discovered, wagons rolled through this and other passes, opening the West to settlement.

The Appalachian Mountains

The Appalachian (ap ə LAY chən) Mountains stretch through eastern North America from Quebec in the north to

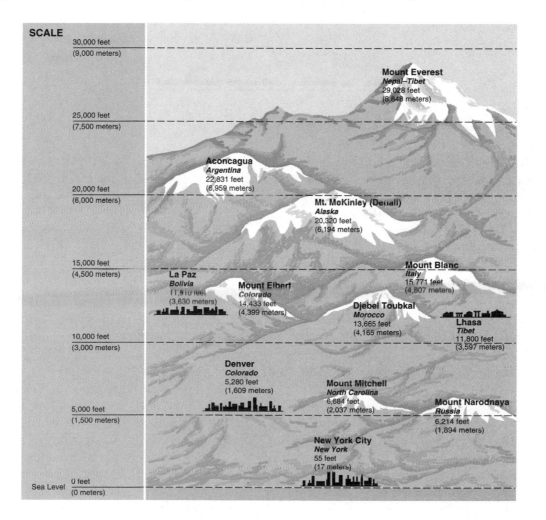

SCALE

30,000 feet (9,000 meters)

25,000 feet (7,500 meters)

20,000 feet (6,000 meters)

15,000 feet (4,500 meters)

10,000 feet (3,000 meters)

5,000 feet (1,500 meters)

Sea Level — 0 feet (0 meters)

Mount Everest
Nepal–Tibet
29,028 feet
(8,848 meters)

Aconcagua
Argentina
22,831 feet
(6,959 meters)

Mt. McKinley (Denali)
Alaska
20,320 feet
(6,194 meters)

Mount Blanc
Italy
15,771 feet
(4,807 meters)

La Paz
Bolivia
11,810 feet
(3,630 meters)

Mount Elbert
Colorado
14,433 feet
(4,399 meters)

Djebel Toubkal
Morocco
13,665 feet
(4,165 meters)

Lhasa
Tibet
11,800 feet
(3,597 meters)

Denver
Colorado
5,280 feet
(1,609 meters)

Mount Mitchell
North Carolina
6,684 feet
(2,037 meters)

Mount Narodnaya
Russia
6,214 feet
(1,894 meters)

New York City
New York
55 feet
(17 meters)

Alabama in the south. This mountain range is more than 1,500 miles (2,400 kilometers) long. The Appalachians are a relatively low range. Their highest point is Mount Mitchell in North Carolina, 6,684 feet (2,037 meters) above sea level.

The Appalachians also stood as a barrier to early pioneers as they tried to settle the continent. In the late 1700s, Daniel Boone led a group of settlers through the Cumberland Gap in Kentucky to open up for settlement the land west of the Appalachians.

Today hikers can walk 2,000 miles (3,200 kilometers) through the range on the Appalachian Trail. This trail is a marked footpath that stretches from Maine to Georgia, running mostly along the crest of the mountains.

The Alaskan Mountains

The Alaskan range includes the highest peak in North America, Mount McKinley, also called Denali. McKinley reaches a height of 20,320 feet (6,194 meters) above sea level. The Alaskan Mountains are truly Arctic mountains. Huge glaciers move down their slopes and fill the valleys with great ice fields. The climate of the range is so threatening that some areas remain unmapped. The Alaskan mountains contain some of the most beautiful scenery in the world. Mount McKinley National Park is in the northern part of the range.

The Andes Mountains

The Andes form the longest mountain chain in the world. It stretches 4,500 miles (7,200 kilometers) from the northern tip to the southern tip of South America along its west coast. The highest peak is Aconcagua (ah kawn KAH gwah), which stands 22,831 feet (6,959 meters) above sea level.

The Andes were formed millions of years ago by a great uplift of the earth's crust. Many active volcanoes in the Andes can still spread disaster when they explode with fire and liquid rock.

The Indians of South America live in many of the high regions of the Andes. Because of the altitude, the air is very thin. The Indians have adapted to their environment over the centuries. They have larger-than-average lungs to take in more air. They also have 20 percent more blood than a lowlander, which allows them to carry more oxygen to their body cells.

The Atlas Mountains

✘ The Atlas range in northwest Africa is rich in legend and history. Ancient Greeks believed that the mountains were the home of the Titan Atlas. Atlas was thought to hold up the heavens on his mighty shoulders. For many centuries, the Atlas Mountains were a mystery because they were impossible to cross.

The people living in the Atlas range have always been proud and independent. The Berber people from the Atlas region swept across North Africa and Spain in the twelfth century. They created an empire that lasted a century. The French gained control of much of northern Africa in the late 1800s. The mountain people, however, resisted their control until the 1930s.

From the north, the Atlas range is especially beautiful. The mountains begin as foothills and then climb higher and higher on the horizon. The highest peak, Djebel Toubkal, reaches 13,665 feet (4,165 meters).

The Alps

The Alps are the largest mountain range in Europe, extending from northern Italy across Austria, the Balkan regions, Switzerland, and France. The highest peak is Mont Blanc, 15,771 feet (4,807 meters) above sea level. The beautiful peaks of the Alps are separated by deep valleys dotted with clear lakes.

✔ Today alpine villages nestle under the towering mountains in scenes out of picture postcards. The beauty of the mountains can suddenly turn to terror, however. In winter and spring, an avalanche is a common occurrence. During an avalanche, tons of snow and ice suddenly break off the mountains and slide into the valleys below. The force of the snow can destroy everything in its path. To protect themselves, villagers plant trees and erect snow fences around their homes. Mountain roads are sheltered by snow sheds. Still, avalanches claim many lives every year in the Alps.

> The Andes form the longest mountain chain in the world.

The Ural Mountains

The Ural Mountains stretch for about 1,500 miles (2,400 kilometers) through Russia and Kazakhstan. The Urals form a north-to-south line that is often considered the dividing point between Europe and Asia. Because the Urals are very old mountains that have been worn down by time, they are of only <u>moderate</u> height. Their rounded hills are generally low and rolling, with steeper slopes on the eastern side. In the north, they average 1,000 to 1,500 feet (305 to 460 meters) high. The highest point is Mount Narodnaya at 6,214 feet (1,894 meters) above sea level.

Much of the Ural range is covered by thick forests. Within the mountains are rich mineral deposits. As early as the 1500s, miners found salt, silver, and gold in the Urals. In the 1800s, the mountains became a famous source of gemstones. Takovaya emeralds are especially prized. During World War II, the Urals supplied the Soviet Union with such valuable resources as iron, copper, asbestos, and potash. Today the Ural range is a leading industrial region.

The Himalaya Mountains

The Himalayas are truly the giants of the earth. They are the highest mountain range in the world. Located in Asia, the Himalayas stretch across parts of Pakistan, India, Kashmir, Tibet, Nepal, Sikkim, and Bhutan. The Himalayas are also the world's youngest mountain range. They are still being pushed higher by earthquakes and other mountain building forces.

The Himalayas are a complex and beautiful group of mountains. There are many famous peaks in the range, but the most famous of all is Everest. Mount Everest is the highest mountain in the world. It reaches an altitude of 29,028 feet (8,848 meters).

The name *Himalaya* comes from the Sanskrit language and means "house of snow." For several different groups of people, the Himalayas are home. In some areas of the mountains, holy men of the Hindu and Buddhist religions live in mountain monasteries. In the Tibetan Himalayas, nomadic tribes live as herders of yaks. Yaks provide them with wool, leather, milk, cheese, meat, and transportation. On the lower slopes of the Himalayas in Nepal, native Sherpas <u>eke</u> out a living as herders and farmers. They have a difficult time raising crops. The farmers cut terraces, like huge steps in the mountainside, to make room for the crops. Rice, wheat, corn, and lentils are the chief terrace crops. They also grow barley, jute, pepper, and tobacco. Sherpas are often among the climbers who attempt to climb Mount Everest.

All the great mountains of the world have now been conquered by mountaineers. Even Everest, the roof of the world, has been scaled.

RECALLING FACTS

1. What happened after a pass was discovered in the Rocky Mountains?

2. One paragraph in the selection is marked with an *X*. Reread that paragraph and underline the sentence that states its main idea.

3. List one similarity between the Rocky Mountains and the Appalachian Mountains.

_____

_____

_____

4. Match each peak in the left column with its mountain range in the right column. Write the letter of the range on the line next to the mountain.

—— Aconcagua   **a.** Alps

—— Everest   **b.** Alaskan Mountains

—— Blanc   **c.** Andes

—— Elbert   **d.** Himalayas

—— McKinley   **e.** Rockies

5. List one similarity and one difference between the Berber tribes and the Sherpa herders.

_____

_____

_____

6. Complete each sentence with the correct word below.

    moderate   **avalanche**   **eke**

a. Actors without acting jobs often

_____ out livings as waiters.

b. A _____ amount of rainfall is neither very great nor very small.

c. The mountain was closed to skiers

because of an _____.

INTERPRETING FACTS

---

1. a. Which of the eight great mountain ranges is farthest north? _____

    b. How does its location affect its climate? _____

_____

2. Why do mountains no longer prevent travel as they used to?

_____

_____

3. Many mountain tribes have lived the same way for hundreds of years. Why might their lives not have changed as much as those of other people?

_____

_____

4. The Himalayas are the world's highest mountain range. They are also the world's youngest mountain range. What effect does time have on mountains?

_____

_____

5. Reread the paragraph with a check mark. Write a sentence stating its main idea.

_____

_____

A. Study the relief map of the Himalayas on page 105. Read the map key. Then answer the questions that follow.

1. How many elevation ranges are shown on this map? _____

2. What is the highest elevation shown? What is the lowest elevation shown?

   _____

3. In what elevation range is Mount Everest? _____

4. Which area has the higher elevation, the Tibetan plain to the north of the Himalayas or

   the Indian plain to the south of the Himalayas? _____

5. In what two countries do the Himalayas reach their greatest height?

   _____

6. Is there any mountain on the map that is not in the same elevation range as Mount

   Everest? _____

B. The elevation illustration on page 103 compares the heights of the highest peak in each of the major mountain ranges. Several cities are also included in the map. Study the elevation scale and the mountain peaks. Then answer the questions that follow.

1. Which mountain shown has the lowest elevation? What is its elevation?

   _____

2. Which mountain has an approximate elevation of 20,000 feet (6,000 meters)?

   _____

3. Which two mountains are close in elevation to Mount Elbert?

   _____

4. What is the approximate difference of elevation between Mount Everest
   and Aconcagua?

   _____

5. Which city shown in the illustration is closest to sea level?

   _____

6. Which city shown in the illustration has the highest elevation?

   _____

7. Which city is closest to the elevation of Mount Mitchell?

   _____

▶ Real Life Connections Research facts about mountain ranges in or near your own state. Which are accessible for climbing? How high is the highest point?

Cause and Effect

Reading a Science Selection

▶ Background Information

Humans have been on Earth for a fraction of its existence. Science only recently has developed the instruments and the methods needed to explore this planet. These modern methods have greatly increased our knowledge of Earth.

Scientists work constantly to explain how the different parts of the earth interact. Scientific theory explains not only what is going on now in the earth. It also describes how the continents and oceans came to be arranged the way that they are, over many millions of years. One theory states that all the continents were once one huge land mass. Such a study sheds light on the land that we live on and the land under the oceans, which cover most of the earth's surface.

However, in the 1950s, scientists studied ocean floors for the first time. They found that they were made of very young rock, which made them question whether all the earth's continents had indeed once been connected.

▶ Skill Focus

The **cause** of an event is the reason it happens. The **effect** is the result of the cause. For example, an earthquake can make a building collapse. The cause is the earthquake. The effect is the collapse of the building.

Sometimes a single cause has many effects. Read the following sentences.

Last night, a fire broke out in our building. Smoke poured out of the upper stories. People ran out into the street. The fire department was alerted.

The cause is the fire. It is given in the first sentence. The effects are given in the next three sentences. Sometimes a single effect has many causes. Read the following sentences.

Janice earned an *A* in science. She often answered the teacher's questions in class. She studied for every test. She did a project for extra credit.

The effect is that Janet earned an *A* in science. It is given in the first sentence. The causes are given in the next three sentences.

Sometimes words signal cause and effect. Look for words, such as *because, cause,* and *as a result.*

▶ Word Clues

Read the sentence below. Look for context clues that explain the underlined word.

Although scientists are certain of the boundaries of the plates, they are dubious about how the plates move.

If you do not know the meaning of the word *dubious,* the word *certain* can help you. *Dubious* and *certain* are antonyms, words that are opposite in meaning. *Dubious* means "not certain."

Use **antonym** context clues to find the meaning of the three underlined words in the selection.

▶ Strategy Tip

As you read the selection, study the diagrams. The labels and captions will help you understand the theories about the movement of the earth's crust.

The Theory of Plate Tectonics

A **theory** (THEE ə ree) is an explanation of observed facts. Scientists base their theories on facts that have been observed or examined. The most recent theory about the movement of the earth's crust is the theory of **plate tectonics** (tek TAHN iks). It begins with the idea that the crust of the earth is made up of seven major plates, or sections, and several smaller plates. These crustal plates make up the topmost, solid part of the earth. The topmost part of the earth is called the **lithosphere** (LITH ə sfir). It covers the floor of the oceans and all the continents.

The seven major lithospheric plates are the Pacific, the North American, the South American, the Eurasian, the African, the Antarctic, and the Australian. The boundaries of the continents are not necessarily the same as the boundaries of the plates. For example, the eastern edge of North America and the western edge of Europe are not the boundaries of plates. The plates that these continents rest on extend into the Atlantic Ocean. These plates include part of the ocean floor.

Two of the smaller plates are the Caribbean and the Arabian. The Arabian plate includes the Arabian Peninsula, the Red Sea, and the Persian Gulf. The Caribbean plate lies between North America and South America.

Although scientists are certain of the boundaries of the plates, they are dubious about how the plates move. The lithospheric plates float like rafts on the **asthenosphere** (as THEN ə sfir). The asthenosphere is made up of hot, liquid rock. The hot liquid and gases flow outward from the inner part of the asthenosphere. This flow of hot, liquid rock below the lithosphere causes the plates to move.

Ocean-Floor Spreading

Midocean ridges are large systems of underwater volcanic mountains. They are found in all the oceans. Deep <u>rifts</u> run through the center of these otherwise solid ridges. When hot, liquid rock flows up from the asthenosphere, it erupts, or explodes upward out of the rifts. This action pushes the plates apart. When the liquid rock, or lava, cools and hardens, new crust is formed. The eruption of lava from between plates can cause the opposite edges of the plates to be pushed down into the asthenosphere. This process is called

Figure 1. This map shows the seven major lithospheric plates and two smaller plates. The Mid-Atlantic Ridge is one of the midocean ridges.

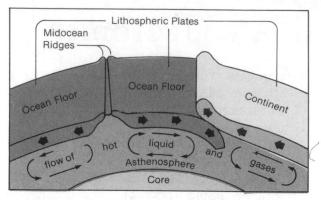

Figure 2. Scientists think that the flow of currents in the asthenosphere causes the movement of lithospheric plates. The boundaries between plates are zones of volcano and earthquake activity.

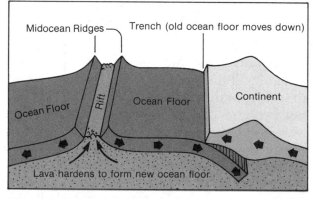

Figure 3. Under the ocean, lava erupts from the rift in the midocean ridge.

ocean-floor spreading. The theory of plate tectonics resulted in part from scientists' discovery of ocean-floor spreading.

In the 1950s, scientists discovered that rocks directly next to the midocean ridges on either side are younger than rocks farther away. The youngest rocks are in the center of the ridges. Based in part on the difference in ages of ocean-floor rocks, scientists believe that new ocean floor is being formed along the ridges. The creation of new ocean floor causes ocean-floor spreading.

Continental Drift

Ocean-floor spreading supports an earlier theory about the movement of the earth's crust. The theory of **continental drift** was first suggested in the early 1900s by a German scientist named Alfred Wegener. Wegener <u>advocated</u> this theory, although most other scientists opposed it. Wegener believed that all the continents were once part of a single landmass. He named the landmass **Pangaea** (pan JEE ə). The landmass broke into separate continents that <u>gradually</u> drifted apart. This did not happen suddenly, but over a long period of time. As a result, there are now seven continents. Many scientists believe that the continents are still drifting.

The theory of plate tectonics is of great interest to scientists today because it helps explain many natural occurrences. For example, earthquakes can be caused by crustal plates sliding past each other, moving apart, or colliding. Volcanic activity and mountain building are also related to such movements. When the plates move apart, hot liquid rock can erupt from the asthenosphere. As the rock cools and hardens, mountains or volcanoes can be formed.

The theory of plate tectonics also combines the ideas of continental drift and ocean-floor spreading.

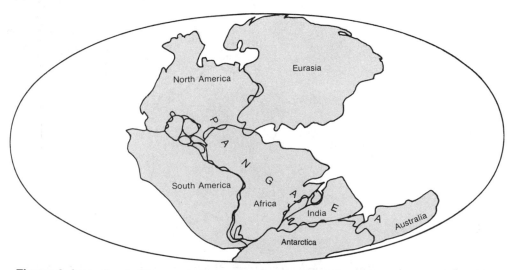

Figure 4. According to Wegener's theory, the continents of the earth were once part of one large landmass. This map shows how the continents may have once been connected.

1. What is a theory?

_____

_____

2. What is the lithosphere?

_____

_____

3. How many major plates are there?

_____

4. What is the asthenosphere made up of?

_____

5. What are midocean ridges?

_____

_____

6. Alfred Wegener developed the theory of

_____ fifty years before scientists found proof of ocean-floor spreading.

7. What natural occurrences can be explained by the movement of crustal plates?

_____

8. Decide if each statement is true or false. Write *true* or *false* on the lines.
   a. A baby's growth from infancy into adulthood is gradual.

   _____

   b. If you advocate building a new library, you are against it.

   _____

   c. Lightning hitting a tree could result in a rift.

   _____

INTERPRETING FACTS

1. The fact that some of the continents look as if they could fit together like a jigsaw puzzle supports the idea that
   a. the continents were once of equal size.
   b. the continents can float on water.
   c. the continents were once joined together.

2. The hot liquid rock and gas in the asthenosphere flows
   a. from a hot area to a cooler area.
   b. from a cold area to a warmer area.
   c. from a high area to a lower area.

3. The volcanic mountains that make up the midocean ridges
   a. are made up of shells and coral.
   b. are made up of the skeletons of deep-sea fish.
   c. are made up of lava from the asthenosphere.

4. The rift in the midocean ridge is a
   a. boundary between crustal plates.
   b. very deep lake.
   c. continental shelf.

5. Ocean-floor spreading does not cause the crustal plates to become larger because
   a. parts of them evaporate.
   b. parts of them are pushed down into the asthenosphere.
   c. parts of them burn up.

1. What in the asthenosphere causes the movement of lithospheric plates?

   _____

   _____

2. What causes the lithospheric plates to be pushed apart?

   _____

3. What was an effect of scientists' discovery of ocean-floor spreading?

   _____

   _____

4. What was the effect of the breakup of Pangaea?

   _____

5. What are three movements of crustal plates that can cause earthquakes?

   _____

   _____

6. What are two effects that can occur when crustal plates move apart?

   _____

   _____

7. Underline two effects of ocean-floor spreading.
   a. heats up the asthenosphere
   b. pushes apart crustal plates
   c. pushes opposite edge of plates down into asthenosphere
   d. causes movement of icebergs
   e. makes oceans deeper

8. What makes scientists believe a new ocean floor is being formed?

   _____

   _____

▶ **Real Life Connections** Research what might have caused a particular geographic feature in your state.

Percents

Reading a Mathematics Selection

▶ Background Information

Percents are an extremely useful mathematical tool to learn. Percents are used in many parts of daily life. A sale at a store claims that you can buy certain items for "15 percent off" the original price. Interest rates on loans and mortgages are stated in percents. When you make up a budget, you often will figure out what percentage of your income you have to spend on each expense.

Much of the information that we get every day from reading and watching television also contains percents. Open up a newspaper, magazine, or book, and you will probably find something about percents. Watch the nightly news on television, and you will see percents are often used to show such information as the rise or fall in the cost of living, the rate of inflation, or the rate of employment. The weatherperson will report that, for example, there is a 20 percent chance of rain tomorrow. If you did not know about percents, you would not understand these different kinds of information.

After reading "Percents" you will have a better understanding of this important and very useful part of mathematics. Because percents are often about money and amounts of goods that are measured in fractions, you will learn in this lesson how to change percents into fractions and decimals, and vice versa.

▶ Skill Focus

The symbol % stands for **percent**. The word *percent* refers to a certain number compared to 100. For example, 83% means 83 parts compared to 100.

Percents are very useful when comparing amounts. For example, you might know that 3 out of every 7 mountains in the world are taller than 8,000 meters and that 5 out of every 9 mountains are snow-covered during the summer. It is difficult, however, to compare these two groups of mountains.

Another way to write 3 out of 7 is 43%. Another way to write 5 out of 9 is 56%. When you compare 43% tall mountains with 56% snow-covered mountains, you can easily see that there

are more snow-covered mountains in summer than mountains that are more than 8,000 meters tall.

Percents can be written as fractions and as decimals. Decimals and fractions can be changed to percents.

▶ Word Clues

The word *percent* comes from two Latin words, *per centum*, meaning "per one hundred or for each hundred." Knowing the meaning of this word will help you understand how to use percents.

When reading the following selection, also look for these important words: *fraction, decimal,* and *change.*

▶ Strategy Tip

Study each section of the selection carefully before going on to the next section. Use the headings to help you understand how the selection is organized.

Reading Percents

The word *percent* refers to a certain number compared to a hundred. Many facts about the mountain systems of the earth can be stated using percentages.

Mountains cover about 20 percent of the earth's surface.

If the earth's surface were divided into 100 equal sections, mountains would cover about 20 of them.

The symbol % stands for percent: 20 percent can be written as 20%. You can think of the percent symbol as two zeros separated by a one. These are the same digits that make up 100.

$$\% = 100$$

Because 20% means 20 out of 100, you can write the same value as the fraction $\frac{20}{100}$. Therefore, 20% and $\frac{20}{100}$ are the same. You can write the fraction $\frac{20}{100}$ as a decimal. Because $\frac{20}{100}$ means 20 one-hundredths, you can write the same value as 0.20. Therefore, 20%, $\frac{20}{100}$, and 0.20 all express the same value.

North America covers about 16 percent of the earth's surface.

16 percent can be written as 16%.

$$16 \text{ out of } 100 = \frac{16}{100}$$

$\frac{16}{100}$ written as a decimal is 0.16.

$$16\% = \frac{16}{100} = 0.16$$

The number in the next example can also be stated as a percent, a fraction, or a decimal.

Approximately 75 percent of the active volcanoes lie in one area of the world.

$$75\% = \frac{75}{100} = 0.75$$

Changing a Percent to a Decimal

To change a percent to a decimal, move the decimal point *two places to the left*. Then remove the % sign.

$$92.6\% = 92.6\% = .926$$

Sometimes you have to put in one or more zeros.

$$3.7\% = 03.7\% = .037$$

Often a decimal point is not shown in the percent. You then have to put a decimal point

at the end of the number and move it two places to the left to make it a decimal.

$$27\% = 27.\% = 0.27$$
$$9\% = 09.\% = .09$$

Changing a Decimal to a Percent

To change a decimal to a percent, move the decimal point *two places to the right*. Then add the % sign.

$$.132 = .132 = 13.2\%$$

Sometimes you have to put in one or more zeros.

$$.7 = .70 = 70\%$$

Sometimes a decimal point is not shown.

$$3 = 3. = 3.00 = 300\%$$
$$17 = 17. = 17.00 = 1700\%$$

Changing a Percent to a Fraction

To change a percent to a fraction, remove the percent sign to form the numerator, and add the denominator 100.

$$93\% = \frac{93}{100}$$

The numerator of this fraction is 93. The denominator of all percent fractions is 100.

$$8\% = \frac{8}{100}$$
$$137\% = \frac{137}{100}$$
$$16\% = \frac{16}{100}$$

Changing a Fraction to a Percent

Two different types of fractions may be changed to a percent. If the denominator of the fraction is 100, just remove the denominator and add a percent sign.

$$\frac{29}{100} = 29\%$$
$$\frac{7}{100} = 7\%$$

If the denominator is not 100, it must first be changed to 100. You need to multiply the numerator and denominator by a number that will change the denominator to 100. For example, to change $\frac{3}{4}$ to a percent, multiply by 25 to change the fraction to $\frac{75}{100}$.

$$\frac{3}{4} = \frac{75}{100} = 75\%$$

To change $\frac{1}{5}$ to a percent, do the following:

$$\frac{1}{5} = \frac{20}{100} = 20\%$$

Study these four rules.

1. To change a percent to a decimal, move the decimal point two places to the *left*. Add a decimal point and zero when they are needed.
2. To change a decimal to a percent, move the decimal point two places to the *right*. Add a decimal point and zeros when they are needed.
3. To change a percent to a fraction, first remove the percent sign. Then put the number over 100.
4. To change a fraction to a percent, remove the denominator if it is 100, and add a percent sign. If the denominator is not 100, multiply the numerator and denominator by a number that will change the denominator to 100. Then add a percent sign to the numerator.

RECALLING FACTS

1. What does the word *percent* mean?

_____

_____

2. What is the symbol for percent?

_____

3. How do you change a percent to a decimal?

_____

_____

_____

_____

4. How do you change a percent to a fraction?

_____

_____

5. How do you change a fraction to a percent?

_____

_____

_____

_____

INTERPRETING FACTS

1. Why does moving the decimal point two places change a percent to a decimal and a decimal to a percent?

_____

_____

2. How might percents be used in ads?

_____

_____

3. Why are percents used to score tests?

_____

4. What part of something is 100% of it?

_____

5. If you had $10 and you earned 100% more, how much would you have all together?

_____

SKILL FOCUS

A. Fill in the blanks. The first one is done for you.

1. 15% = $\frac{15}{100}$ = .15
2. 13% = _____ = _____
3. 137% = _____ = _____
4. 36% = _____ = _____
5. 8%   = _____ = _____

6. 34.7% = _____ = _____
7. 1.1% = _____ = _____
8. 3%   = _____ = _____
9. 75%   = _____ = _____
10. 50% = _____ = _____

B. Change the percents to decimals and the decimals to percents.

1. 14%   = _____
2. 73%   = _____
3. 5%   = _____
4. 100% = _____
5. 83.9% = _____

6. .16 = _____
7. .84 = _____
8. .03 = _____
9. 1.04 = _____
10. .752 = _____

C. Change the fractions to percents and the percents to fractions.

1. $\frac{79}{100}$ = _____
2. $\frac{7}{100}$ = _____
3. $\frac{3.7}{100}$ = _____
4. $\frac{1}{4}$ = _____
5. $\frac{3}{5}$ = _____

6. 67% = _____
7. 29% = _____
8. 2%   = _____
9. 125% = _____
10. 43% = _____

D. Write the percent, fraction, and decimal for the following amounts.

1. Twenty-five and nine tenths percent. _____
2. Eight twenty-fifths _____
3. Twelve tenths _____
4. Forty-two hundredths _____

▶ **Real Life Connections** Where do you read percents in your daily life?

Evaluating Opinions

What is the difference between a fact and an opinion? A fact is a statement that can be checked and proven. An opinion is a statement that tells how someone feels or what someone thinks about something. Some opinions may be more sound than others because they have one or more facts to back them up. When you find an opinion in your reading, decide whether it is sound.

Read the following selection.

The Sierra Nevada is a huge mountain range in eastern California. Sierra Nevada means "snowy, saw-toothed mountain" in Spanish. The Sierra Nevada is the site of three national parks—Yosemite, Sequoia, and Kings Canyon—and beautiful Lake Tahoe. Donner Memorial State Park, a historic landmark, is also in this mountain range.

The Sierra Nevada is like a granite wall extending north and south for 430 miles (692 kilometers) through California. It is about 70 miles (110 kilometers) wide. At one time, the earth's crust lifted and tilted to the west to make a long gentle slope on the mountain's western side and a steep slope on its eastern side. The highest point of the Sierra Nevada is Mt. Whitney. Its altitude, or height, is 14,494 feet (4,418 meters). In fact, Mt. Whitney is the second highest point in the United States. Several other peaks of the Sierra Nevada are close to the height of Mt. Whitney.

Rivers, such as the Feather, American, and San Joaquin, flow in the Sierra Nevada. Rushing mountain waters have cut deep canyons in the long western slope of the mountain range. Yosemite Valley is the most outstanding of these canyons. Yosemite was originally cut by streams. Later, glaciers moved down the valley, eroding it further. The glaciers created the Sierra Nevada's granite cliffs and impressive landscapes. On the shorter, steeper eastern slope, many creeks descend and join the Owens, Walker, Carson, and Truckee rivers. The cliffs, meadows, evergreen forests, lakes, and waterfalls make the Sierra Nevada a beautiful mountain range.

The higher up the mountain range, the greater the rainfall. This is true up to 4,500 feet (1,350 meters). From there to the top, the rain decreases. In a typical winter, 30 to 40 feet (9 to 12 meters) of snow accumulates at Lake Tahoe and Donner Pass, but as much as 60 feet (18 meters) of snow can fall. It is no wonder that skiers are attracted to this region.

A variety of vegetation grows on the Sierra Nevada at different elevations. Shrubs and grasses grow near the Sacramento and San Joaquin valleys at the western base of the Sierra Nevada. From 3,000 to 4,000 feet (900 to 1,200 meters) are forests of yellow pine, sugar pine, cedar, and fir. These trees are a valuable source of timber. Within the forest is the *Sequoia gigantea,* or "big tree." This is the largest plant on the earth. At 6,000 to 7,000 feet (1,800 to 2,150 meters), lodgepole pine, Jeffrey pine, and red fir grow. Above the timberline is rocky land that is barren except for scattered evergreens. The rivers of the western slope of the mountain range supply water for irrigation. The farms in the Sacramento and San Joaquin valleys and the Tulare Basin receive this water. The largest cities in California receive their water supply from these rivers, too. Hydroelectric plants on the rivers generate the power for farmlands and cities.

The Sierra Nevada forms a barrier to east-west travel. Cars, trucks, and buses can cross the mountains through several passes. Major highways use six passes, each at a different elevation. A road at 9,625 feet (2,935 meters) over Tioga Pass connects Yosemite Valley and Mono Lake. But this road is usually closed nine months of the year because of snow. Railroads travel over the Sierra Nevada. Hikers and pack trains, or groups of mules, use the various trails to cross the mountain range.

The gold rush of 1849 began when gold was discovered in the Sierra Nevada. This attracted many people to the foothill region in the 1800s. Mining of gold and other metals is no longer important. Now tourism is the area's chief industry. All kinds of camping and recreational facilities are located throughout the Sierra Nevada for people who enjoy summer or winter sports. Other industry in the region includes fruit-growing, lumbering, and grazing.

Read the opinions about the Sierra Nevada in the left column. Select none, one, or two of the facts in the right column that support each opinion. Write the letter of each supporting fact on the line before the opinion. Leave the line blank if the opinion has no supporting facts.

1. _____ The Sierra Nevada is a huge mountain range.

2. _____ The Sierra Nevada is the nation's best recreation area.

3. _____ Lake Tahoe is one of the most beautiful lakes in the world.

4. _____ Yosemite Valley is the most outstanding canyon in the United States.

5. _____ The Sierra Nevada is a beautiful mountain range.

6. _____ The best skiing in the West is in the Sierra Nevada.

7. _____ No forests can offer as large a selection of timber as those of the Sierra Nevada.

8. _____ A better road is needed over Tioga Pass.

9. _____ Visitors to California should spend their time seeing the Sierra Nevada rather than Disneyland.

10. _____ Some of the best fruit in the United States is grown in the Sierra Nevada.

11. _____ If not for the rivers of the Sierra Nevada, California would be without water.

12. _____ Mt. Whitney seems very high.

13. _____ There is no need for trails for pack trains.

a. Each year, the Sierra Nevada receives 30 to 40 feet (9 to 12 meters) of snow.

b. The range has meadows, cliffs, and forests.

c. At 4,000 feet (1,200 meters) is yellow pine, sugar pine, cedar, and fir.

d. The Sierra Nevada is over 400 miles (640 kilometers) long.

e. It is the site of three national parks.

f. Rivers on the western slope supply California's largest cities with water.

g. The Sierra Nevada is about 70 miles (110 kilometers) wide.

h. Some winters, 60 feet (18 meters) of snow fall.

i. Glaciers moved down the Yosemite Valley and created cliffs and impressive landscapes.

j. The peak of Mt. Whitney is 14,494 feet (4,418 meters) high.

k. Rivers on the western slope irrigate farmlands.

l. Heavy snow at Tioga Pass keeps it closed nine months out of the year.

m. At 7,000 feet (2,150 meters) is lodgepole pine, Jeffrey pine, and red fir.

n. The range has waterfalls, such as those in Yosemite Valley.

Improving Reading Rate

People have so much to read today that the ability to read quickly has become important. The typical reader of a century ago had fewer books, newspapers, and magazines to read. For this reason, you may read more in a week than your great-grandparents did. Being able to read rapidly helps you to read more in a short period of time. However, it is always important to keep in mind that to read material without understanding it is a waste of time no matter what the speed.

A rapid rate of reading has no particular value in itself. A good reader is able to read at several speeds depending on the material being read. When reading materials are difficult or unfamiliar, a good reader reads slower. For example, social studies, science, and mathematics may be more difficult to read than literature. So these materials are read more slowly. Even literature can be difficult. Sometimes a reader needs to reread a paragraph to understand a complex idea. A good reader needs to slow down when words or sentences are difficult or unfamiliar. A good reader also stops to read diagrams and maps. This requires increased attention, making a slower reading rate necessary.

The first thing to do to increase your reading rate is to get rid of bad reading habits. Any of the habits listed below will prevent you from increasing your reading rate.

To answer each question, write *yes* or *no* on the line provided.

_____ **1.** Do you move your lips when reading silently?

_____ **2.** Do you point to words with your finger as you read?

_____ **3.** Do you move your head from side to side as you read?

_____ **4.** Do you read one word at a time?

Perhaps you have been doing some of these things for years. If so, it may take you some time to overcome them. But it can be done if you try. If you have any of these habits, practice the suggestions below for overcoming them.

Lip moving	Hold your finger over your lips, or hold a piece of paper between your lips.
Finger pointing	Hold your book with both hands, one on each side of the book.
Head moving	Rest your chin in the palm of one hand and hold it still.
Reading one word at a time	Work hard at trying to take in several words at each glance.

The following paragraph is marked off into word groups. See if you can read it by taking in each group of words in one glance.

Bertela lives / on an island / that belongs / to Denmark. / There are / beech trees / in the woods / near her home. / Every fall / she gathers beech nuts / in these woods. / The squirrels gather / the nuts, too. / The nuts are so plentiful / that there are / enough of them / for both Bertela / and the squirrels.

Below is a selection that can be used in checking your reading rate. Use a watch or a clock with a second hand to time yourself. Start right on a minute, such as four minutes past ten o'clock. Write your starting time at the beginning of the selection. Then read the selection. Write your ending time at the end of the selection.

Starting time _____

The Mistake

At the top of the hill, the three riders reined their horses to a stop. They wore blue coats, tan trousers, high boots, and three-cornered hats. The tallest of the riders lifted a pair of field glasses to his eyes and looked out over the fields and woods.

"Tell us, General Washington, what do you see? British soldiers? campfires?" asked one of the riders.

Washington smiled. "Remember, Lafayette, it will take the British a few days to reach this area from the Delaware River."

Lafayette looked disappointed. Then General Greene, the third rider, spoke. "General Washington, we have ridden all over this land today, and we still have not found a good place for battle against the British."

"True enough," Washington sighed.

Greene looked up at the darkening sky. "Look, sir, it's going to storm."

The three riders started toward a field below them. Black clouds raced across the sky. It began to thunder.

"There's a house ahead!" shouted Lafayette. "Let's stop there."

"Yes, hurry!" Washington led the dash to the farmhouse.

Just as the riders reached the barn near the house, the rain came pouring down. They got off their horses and looked around. A farmer was staring at them. "Why, it's General George Washington. Here on my farm! General, sir, welcome. Come into my house and have some food. My son Tom will look after your horses. Our name is Small."

Washington smiled and went into the house with the farmer. Lafayette followed the general. But Greene stayed with the horses. He was worried. Suppose these were friends of the British. The boy might hide their horses, and they would be trapped. Finally, however, he decided to follow the others.

Inside the warm house, Washington sat at the table talking with the farmer. Lafayette was pacing from window to window. Washington looked out the window and said, "Mr. Small, I see this storm will last for hours. I wonder if you would let us stay the night?"

Both Lafayette and Greene looked worried. Greene whispered to the general, "Sir, we can't stay. We don't know if these people are friends or enemies. We might be in British hands by morning!"

Washington said coldly, "We will stay."

Dinner was good, and even Greene enjoyed it. For a while, he felt at ease and almost forgot his fears. Lafayette also seemed to relax and was talking a mile a minute. But when they went upstairs, all of Greene's fears returned. Without undressing, he lay on top of the bed with his gun at his side and his eyes open. He jumped up with each new sound.

Just before sunrise, Greene heard a horse whinny and a dog bark. Silently he went downstairs and out to the barn. The horses seemed safe. He put his hand on his gray horse.

"Don't do it, sir." A low voice cut the darkness.

"Who's there?" His hand on his gun, Greene whirled around.

"Me! Tom Small! And I say don't run away. The general needs you."

"Run away? What do you mean?" asked Greene.

Tom looked at his feet. "I've been standing watch because I was afraid you were going to slip away with your horse."

"Fool!" shouted Greene. "You think me a traitor?"

Tom looked uneasy. "Well, you acted so strange, sir. I just thought . . . There have been lots of deserters—traitors, too."

Suddenly Greene laughed. "Tom, we're a pair! We both were worried about the same thing. I came down here because I heard some noise and thought the British had trapped us."

Two hours later at breakfast, Washington looked at Greene and said, "You look like you didn't sleep all night. What's wrong?"

Greene winked at Tom. "Nothing, sir. Tom and I just stood watch all night."

Washington looked from one to the other but said nothing. Later, after they had left the Smalls', they stopped to rest. Washington broke the silence. "You know, you were right. I did take a risk last night. I was quite wrong."

Greene could only nod. But Lafayette held out his hand to Washington. "Ah, my general, only a great man will say, 'I was wrong.'"

To find the total time that it took to read the selection, do the following: (1) Subtract your beginning time from your ending time. (2) Divide the number of words in the selection by the remainder expressed in seconds. If it took you 3 minutes and 5 seconds ($3 \times 60 + 5 = 185$ seconds) to read the selection, you would have read 3.7 words per second ($695 \div 185 = 3.7$). (3) To find the number of words per minute (WPM), multiply your rate per second by 60. Your answer would be 222 WPM.

Words in selection: 695

	Hr.	Min.	Sec.
Ending time:	____	____	____
Starting time:	____	____	00
Total time:	____	____	____

No. words: 695 = ____ × 60 = ____ WPM

No. seconds: _____

To check your understanding of the selection, fill in the circle in front of the correct answer to each question.

1. Where did the three riders stop the first time?
   ○ **a.** at a farmhouse
   ○ **b.** under a tree
   ○ **c.** at the top of a hill

2. Who looked through the field glasses?
   ○ **a.** General Greene
   ○ **b.** General Washington
   ○ **c.** Lafayette

3. Where does the farmer greet the general?
   ○ **a.** in his house
   ○ **b.** at his barn
   ○ **c.** in the field

4. Who looks after the riders' horses?
   ○ **a.** General Greene
   ○ **b.** General Washington
   ○ **c.** Tom Small

5. Why is Lafayette pacing from window to window?
   ○ **a.** He is hungry.
   ○ **b.** He is afraid of thunder.
   ○ **c.** He is worried about the British.

6. Which of the three riders seems to enjoy his stay with the Smalls?
   ○ **a.** General Greene
   ○ **b.** General Washington
   ○ **c.** Lafayette

7. How do you know that Greene did not sleep very much at the Smalls'?
   ○ **a.** He doesn't undress.
   ○ **b.** He has his gun at his side.
   ○ **c.** He keeps his eyes open.

8. Why does Greene go down to the barn?
   ○ **a.** He hears some noises.
   ○ **b.** He wants to talk to Tom.
   ○ **c.** He can't sleep.

9. Why does Tom stay up all night?
   ○ **a.** He is afraid the British will come.
   ○ **b.** He can't sleep.
   ○ **c.** He thinks Greene might run away.

10. What does Tom mean when he says, "There have been lots of deserters …"?
    ○ **a.** Many U.S. soldiers stole horses.
    ○ **b.** Many farmers hid U.S. soldiers.
    ○ **c.** Many U.S. soldiers ran away.

Lesson 39

Taking Notes

When reading new information that you need to remember, it is a good idea to take notes. **Taking notes** will help you remember the information as you read it. Taking notes is especially helpful in recording the information from several references before writing a report.

Not everything you read is necessary to remember. When taking notes, write down only the important information, especially main ideas and supporting details. Following are some suggestions to help you take notes.

1. Find the main idea of each paragraph and include it in your notes.
2. Look for major details that answer such questions as *who, what, when, why,* and *how.* Write these details under the main ideas. Leave out minor details, or information that is not needed.
3. Arrange your notes in the same order in which the information appears in the selection. Group each main idea and its supporting details together.
4. Label your notes by writing the subject at the top of the page. Write your notes in your own words. Do not copy entire sentences, but write down key words and phrases. Be brief so that you can read your notes quickly.

The following selection is written in chronological order, the order in which the events take place. Using the space provided on page 123, take notes as you read the selection. Make sure your notes show the sequence of the visits of the Spanish explorers to the New World.

Explorations to the New World

Columbus's voyages to the New World led the way to further exploration of North and South America. By the Treaty of Tordesillas, Spain claimed the right to most of the New World. Early Spanish explorers heard stories of wealthy kingdoms in the Americas. Such reports encouraged new expeditions. Until 1519, Spanish control of the New World was limited to small settlements in the West Indies. With the many Spanish expeditions that followed Columbus, Spain gradually gained control of most of South and Central America and parts of North America.

Hernando Cortés

In 1519, Hernando Cortés, a clever fighter and skillful leader, landed on the coast of Mexico in search of gold. He soon heard about the powerful Aztec Empire that demanded huge payments from the people it conquered. Cortés sought out the support of the many Indian tribes who hated their Aztec rulers. He marched his small army of 400 soldiers and 16 horses into the crowded Aztec capital of Tenochtitlan where he confronted the Aztec ruler Montezuma.

After months of negotiations, Montezuma agreed to become a subject of the Spanish king. In 1520, the Aztecs revolted against the Spanish. Cortés and his army barely escaped with their lives. However, with the help of his allies, Cortés surrounded Tenochtitlan. In 1521, he attacked and destroyed the Aztec capital. Within a few years, the Aztec Empire crumbled.

Francisco Pizarro

Nine years later, in 1530, Francisco Pizarro, another explorer, received permission to explore the Inca Empire of present-day Peru. With 180 metal-clad soldiers—less than half of Cortés's force—Pizarro marched into the Andean kingdom. Luck was with him. When he arrived, the Incas were caught up in a civil war.

Pizarro launched a surprise attack, imprisoned the Inca leader Atahualpa, and killed most of his attendants. The attack stunned the Incas, weakening their resistance to the Spanish. By 1535, Pizarro had captured Cuzco, the Inca capital, and crushed nearly all opposition.

Francisco Coronado

In 1540, Francisco Coronado led an expedition in search of the "seven cities of gold" reportedly nestled in the hills of present-day New Mexico. For about two years, Coronado, along with many Spanish soldiers, searched in vain for these cities of gold that did not really exist. In the process, he explored much of the future southwestern United States. One of his lieutenants was the first European to see the Grand Canyon.

Hernando de Soto

While Coronado was looking for gold in the west, Hernando de Soto led another gold-hunting expedition into what would become the southeastern United States. From 1539 to 1542, his army wandered as far north as the Carolinas and as far west as present-day Oklahoma. When de Soto died, the expedition returned without finding any large supplies of gold. Even before de Soto's death, the Spanish had begun to concentrate on settling the area to the south, in present-day Mexico, the Caribbean, and South America.

Early Exploration

_____

_____

_____

_____

_____

_____

_____

_____

Taking notes can help you remember and review what you have read. Use the information from your notes to complete the chart. The first explorer has been started for you.

Explorer	Areas Explored	Dates	Importance
Cortés			

Reading a Road Map

Whether you are driving to a park across town or to a scenic spot across the country, it is a good idea to have a road map with you. A road map shows how to get from one place to another and how far it is between places. It also shows the location of points of interest.

The road map below shows the Great Smoky Mountains National Park and some of the surrounding areas.

Notice the key to the right of the map. A key explains the symbols used on a map. The scale of miles helps you figure out the distance from one place to another. The road classification symbols identify different kinds of roads. Special symbols also mark such features as towns, campgrounds, ski areas, and other points of interest. Maps usually include a direction symbol known as a compass. The compass indicates north, south, east, and west with the abbreviations N, S, E, and W.

A. Read the definitions in the left column. Then read the words in the right column. On the line next to each definition, write the correct word.

1. _____ explains map symbols   scale of miles

2. _____ indicates directions   road classification

3. _____ shows distance from one place to another   key

4. _____ identifies different kinds of roads   special features

5. _____ campgrounds, ski areas, mountains   compass

B. Decide if each of the following questions can be answered using the map on the opposite page. Write *yes* or *no* on the line.

_____ 1. Are there hiking trails in Great Smoky Mountains National Park?

_____ 2. What towns are south of the park?

_____ 3. How long does it take to drive through the park?

_____ 4. Are there campgrounds inside the park itself?

_____ 5. Are there hotels and motels near the park?

_____ 6. Which roads are closed in the winter?

_____ 7. Which rivers run through the park?

_____ 8. How high is Newfound Gap?

_____ 9. How many miles is it from the park to New York City?

_____ 10. How do you get from Gatlinburg to the Cherokee Indian Reservation?

_____ 11. Is fishing permitted in the park?

_____ 12. Are there any gravel roads in the park?

_____ 13. If you leave Gatlinburg at 9:00 A.M., when will you get to Mt. Le Conte?

C. Fill in the circle next to the phrase that correctly completes each sentence.

1. The Great Smoky Mountains National Park is in the states of
   ○ North Carolina and South Carolina.
   ○ Tennessee and North Carolina.
   ○ Tennessee and Kentucky.

2. If you travel south through the park from Gatlinburg, you will first reach
   ○ Park Headquarters and Sugarland Visitors Center.
   ○ Newfound Gap.
   ○ Smokemont Campground.

3. To get from Gatlinburg to Cosby, you can travel on
   ○ US 441.   ○ Route 339.   ○ US 321.

4. The Interstate Highway that is closest to the park is
   ○ Interstate 82.   ○ Interstate 75.   ○ Interstate 40.

5. The highest point in Tennessee is
   ○ Newfound Gap.   ○ Clingman's Dome.   ○ Mt. Le Conte.

6. The trail that goes from the western part of the park to the eastern part is
   ○ the Appalachian Trail.   ○ the Gatlinburg Trail.   ○ the Forney Ridge Trail.

7. A large body of water on the southern border of the park is called
   ○ Rainbow Falls.   ○ Fontana Lake.   ○ Forney Creek.

8. When going from Newfound Gap to Smokemont Campground, you would travel
   ○ southwest.   ○ northwest.   ○ southeast.

Lesson 41

Conflict and Resolution

Reading a Literature Selection

▶ Background Information

Training for an Olympic sport demands a lot from competitors. These athletes must either commit themselves totally to their sports or risk failure. This play is about a young woman who must make a decision that will affect her life for several years. Can she commit herself to years of working hard and practicing constantly?

▶ Skill Focus

Often the characters in a story have a goal to achieve or a problem to solve. The struggle to achieve the goal or solve the problem is called **conflict**.

A character can face three main types of conflict.

Conflict with Self

A character may struggle with emotions or feelings within himself or herself. This struggle is an internal conflict. An example is a person trying to overcome a fear of high places.

Conflict with Another Character

A character may struggle against another person. This struggle is an external, or outside, conflict. An example is two marathon, or long-distance, runners competing for a place on the U.S. Olympic Team.

Conflict with an Outside Force

A character may struggle against nature, society, or some danger over which he or she has no control. This struggle is also an external conflict. An example is a firefighter battling flames to save people inside a burning building.

By the end of a story, the character facing a conflict succeeds or fails in achieving the goal or solving the problem. The way a conflict is settled is called the **resolution**. Conflict and resolution are part of a story's plot, or main action.

Stories sometimes have more than one conflict. As you read, look for conflicts and their resolutions.

▶ Word Clues

Often when you read, you may find words that you don't know because they are not part of your experience. Read the following sentence.

> Besides, my eyes are always red from the <u>chlorine</u> in the pool.

You can tell from the context clues that *chlorine* is something in the pool. However, there are no context clues to tell you what chlorine is. You will need a **dictionary** to help you. You may find it more convenient to finish what you are reading first and then look up the word.

Use a dictionary to find the meaning of the four underlined words in the play.

▶ Strategy Tip

As you read the play, be alert to the playwright's use of dialogue, scene changes, and stage directions. Also notice how the main conflict develops. Remember to look for other conflicts in addition to the main conflict of the story.

The Campaign for Kate

Cast
Kate Fenton, member of a swim team
Maria Cortez, member of a swim team
Mr. Meacham, coach of the swim team

Scene 1

Late in the afternoon at the Hillside High School pool. Mr. Meacham stands at the edge of the pool, stopwatch in hand. When Mr. Meacham speaks, the team stops doing laps. Everyone leaves the pool but Kate and Maria, who hang on to the edge and talk.

Mr. Meacham *(loudly):* All right, team, that's enough for today. I'll see you all tomorrow, bright and early. Remember, be here no later than 6:30 A.M.

Kate *(to Maria):* He'll see me, but I won't see him. I'll be swimming, but I'll probably nap through my first four laps! I don't know if I can keep this up.

Maria: Mr. Meacham says it's important to work out every day for several hours, especially with the all-county meet coming up Saturday.

Kate: Well, I'm beginning to get tired of this stuff. Besides, my eyes are always red from the chlorine in the pool. And it doesn't do my hair

any good, either. And furthermore, practicing five hours a day doesn't leave me time or energy for anything else. And for what—so I can someday say I'm a great swimmer in the <u>butterfly</u> event?

Maria: I know; I'm tired, too. But now I take Mr. Meacham's advice and go to bed an hour earlier. Maybe you should try that.

Kate: Agh! I go to bed early as it is. I need some time to myself, to do other things. If I go to bed any earlier I'll sleep away my whole life. You know, I used to love swimming. I had dreams *(pause)* . . . dreams of becoming an Olympic champion like Summer Sanders or Qian Hong. Now it's more like a nightmare than a dream.

Maria: I heard Mr. Meacham say you have the talent to make the Olympic team some day.

Kate: He did—but I keep wondering if I can throw myself into swimming and train the way he wants me to. I don't know if I'm ready to give up everything just to try for it.

Maria: Here comes Mr. Meacham. We'd better talk about this later.

Mr. Meacham *(very enthusiastic):* Good workout, Maria. Your time is improving. *(turns toward Kate, showing concern)* Kate, you've just got to think about your kick as you finish each lap. It's cutting down your speed. You could lose a race that way. Tomorrow morning we'll work on it. I think you're either daydreaming or not getting enough sleep.

Kate: I'll be all right, Mr. Meacham.

Mr. Meacham: Well, you'd better hit the showers and then go home to hit the books. I want my team to get decent grades, too!

Kate and Maria clamber out of the pool and head for the showers.

Kate *(takes off her swimming cap):* By the way, some of the kids want me to run for the student senate. What do you think?

Maria *(throws a towel over her shoulders):* It sounds great, but do you have the time? Mr. Meacham says swimming has top priority.

Kate: I'll just have to make the time. Anyway, Maria, you take Mr. Meacham too seriously. Just because you want to be a swim coach someday.

Maria: I have to work harder than you, Kate! *(getting angry)* You have a natural talent that I could never match. I'll be glad if I can be a coach someday . . . You can set your sights even higher. I get angry when you won't!

Kate: OK! OK! Sorry. Friends?

Maria *(pause):* Friends.

Scene 2

Saturday. Kate and Maria sit on a bench in the locker room before the swim meet begins.

Maria *(concerned):* You look tired, Kate.

Kate *(fatigue shows in her voice):* I'm beat. I was at a campaign meeting last night until all hours. We were painting posters and writing slogans. How does this one sound? "Get in the swim—Vote for Kate!"

Maria: Sounds great. I love slogans. They can say a lot in a few words. They can appeal to emotions and make something popular. Now let's get in the swim ourselves. Let's go out there so you can beat me and everyone else without even trying, as usual!

Kate and Maria rise and walk toward the locker room doors.

Scene 3

Maria and Kate cling to the edge of the pool after the race.

Kate *(in spite of her disappointment):* Congratulations, Maria! First place, and your best time ever! You even beat my best time!

Maria *(happy and relieved):* I can hardly believe it myself, beating you and everyone else in the pool! I've never done that before!

Kate: You deserve it; you work hard, Maria.

Mr. Meacham *(walks toward Maria and Kate):* Maria! That was great! Congratulations! *(turns to Kate)* Now Kate. *(becomes very serious)* I want to talk to you. You've got to work on your kick as you make the turn.

Kate *(raises her voice, becomes angry):* Mr. Meacham, can't you leave me alone? I hate my kick! I hate this pool! I'm not meant for this. Some Olympic athlete! I can't even win a high school race! *(gets out of the pool and walks over to the starter's table)*

Mr. Meacham *(follows Kate):* You certainly won't make the Olympic team with that attitude.

Kate: Well, you saw today that I haven't got what it takes.

Mr. Meacham *(very calmly):* All I saw today was a swimmer who wasn't concentrating. Kate, you have a natural talent. It's far greater than that of any other member of the team. Maria knows it. Today was a lucky break for her. It may not come again. Maria knows her best shot is to study to be a coach. But you could be a star if you work to develop your talent.

Kate: I don't know if I can work that hard at swimming. You said it was important to be well rounded. Some kids want me to run for a place as representative in the student government. On a day like today, that sounds like a good idea. Why shouldn't I do it?

Mr. Meacham (*very patiently*): For most kids, it would be a great idea. But your talent is special, Kate. You shouldn't give up your chance at an Olympic medal someday because you spread yourself too thin. (*pause*) I have an idea. You continue to come to practice, but don't compete for the next three weeks. Run for the student senate. But you must make up your mind by the end of the three weeks. If you decide to swim in the meet on the fourteenth, you've committed yourself to swimming. If you don't race on the fourteenth, you're off the team.

Kate: OK. (*walks slowly toward the locker room*) I can accept that.

Scene 4

The following week. Kate and Maria chat in the pool.

Maria: Did you hear, Kate? I won again yesterday! Our whole team won.

Kate: I heard, I heard! Mr. Meacham must be pleased.

Maria: Oh, sure. But he misses you. I even miss swimming four strokes behind you!

Kate: Maria, you put yourself down too much. You work hard. You deserve to win.

Maria: Speaking of winning, how is your campaign coming?

Kate: I have until the fourteenth to officially begin my campaign.

Maria: That's the day of the next race!

Kate: I know, I know.

Kate and Maria swim to the end of the pool to start their laps.

Scene 5

The fourteenth. Hillside High School pool, less than 20 minutes before the swim meet. Kate is nowhere in sight.

Mr. Meacham: Maria, have you seen Kate? Is she coming?

Maria (*sits on the bench near the locker room door*): I don't know. Last night on the phone she said something about showing us her new campaign posters.

Mr. Meacham (*his disappointment is obvious*): Then she's decided.

Kate (*bursts into the pool area*): I thought you'd like to take a look at these. Here's one for you, coach. (*Mr. Meacham slowly takes the poster from Kate*) And one for you, Maria.

Maria (*eagerly reads*): "Get in the swim with Kate—and vote for someone else!"

Mr. Meacham: Great Kate! Let's get ready for the Olympics!

Curtain

RECALLING FACTS

1. Who is the main character in this play?

   _____

2. How is Kate's goal different from Maria's?

   _____

   _____

   _____

   _____

3. Why does Maria feel she is not as good a swimmer as Kate?

   _____

   _____

4. Why is Kate so tired the day of the first swim meet?

   _____

   _____

   _____

   _____

5. What does Mr. Meacham say was the cause of Kate's loss at the swim meet?

   _____

   _____

   _____

6. Why does Kate tell Maria that she deserves to win first place?

_____

_____

_____

7. Fill in the circle in front of the word that correctly completes each sentence.

a. Something thought of as being more important than something else is a _____.

○ lap   ○ campaign   ○ priority

b. Someone swimming on his or her stomach combining a kick and double overarm pull is doing the _____.

○ butterfly   ○ side stroke   ○ crawl

c. Very young children _____ on a jungle gym.

○ swim   ○ clamber   ○ somersault

d. Someone who is extremely tired is suffering from a feeling of _____

○ fatigue   ○ disgust   ○ failure

INTERPRETING FACTS

1. How are Maria and Kate different?

_____

_____

_____

2. If Kate and Maria are friends, why do they argue?

_____

_____

3. Why is training as a swimmer so demanding?

_____

_____

4. How do you think Kate felt when she heard about Maria's second victory?

_____

_____

5. From the stage directions in Mr. Meacham's dialogue, what kind of person do you think Mr. Meacham is?

_____

_____

_____

6. What is the message of this play?

_____

_____

Think about the conflict Kate faced and how she solved it. Then answer these questions.

1. Of the three conflicts described at the beginning of the lesson, which conflict did Kate face?

_____

2. What was Kate's conflict? _____

_____

_____

3. How did Mr. Meacham, the coach, help Kate with her problem?

_____

_____

_____

4. How was the conflict finally resolved? _____

_____

_____

5. Was Kate's conflict internal or external? Explain.

_____

_____

6. There is also a minor conflict in the story. It is an external conflict. Circle the letter of the statement that identifies this minor conflict. Then tell how it was resolved.
   a. Maria had to deal with being second best.
   b. Maria got angry with Kate over her unwillingness to work hard.
   c. Maria did not get along with her coach.

_____

_____

7. Maria also has a conflict with herself about her love of swimming and her knowledge that she is not a first-class swimmer. How does she resolve this conflict?

_____

_____

8. How does the title of this play, "The Campaign for Kate," have two meanings?

_____

_____

▶ Real Life Connections Describe a recent conflict in your life. How did you resolve it?

Reading a Timeline

Reading a Social Studies Selection

▶ Background Information

The Olympic Games are the biggest sporting event in the world. Competitors from around the world come together to compete in various sports. These athletes are the best at what they do.

Almost everyone has an Olympic memory. You may remember Michael Jordan and the "Dream Team" winning the gold medal in basketball, or Nancy Kerrigan skating her way to the silver medal in figure skating in 1994.

While you probably have watched the Olympics on television, you may not know about the history of the Olympics.

The history of the Olympic Games can be divided into two parts. The games began in ancient Greece, even before recorded history. These games went on, uninterrupted, for 1,200 years, until they were ended by the Roman emperor Theodosius (thee ə DOH shee əs). The games were not played again until 1896, when the modern Olympic Games began. They have continued to this time.

This selection describes the early Olympics in ancient Greece. It also describes the revival of the games in 1896. The timeline on pages 133 and 134 presents information not included in the text.

▶ Skill Focus

Historical events are usually studied in chronological order. Chronological order is the order in which events take place. In addition to describing historical events in paragraphs, textbooks sometimes use **timelines** to show the sequence of events.

A timeline is a kind of graph of events in chronological order. Each section on a timeline stands for a certain period of time— one year, ten years, a century, or some other length of time. The timeline shows the important events that occurred in each time period.

A timeline shows information in a brief, clear form. It helps you understand when an event happened in relation to other events. A timeline also gives you a quick overview of the history of a particular region, topic, or period.

▶ Word Clues

Read the sentence that follows. Look for context clues that explain the underlined word.

The Olympics started in ancient Greece so long ago that their origin, or beginning, is not recorded in history.

If you don't know the meaning of the word *origin,* the word following the word *or* can help you. An origin is a beginning. The word *origin* is explained in this appositive phrase set off by a comma. An appositive phrase gives the meaning of the word that comes right before it.

Use **appositive** phrases to find the meaning of the three underlined words in the selection.

▶ Strategy Tip

Before you read "Swifter, Higher, Stronger," preview it. The headings and the timeline give you an overview of the games from ancient Greece to today. Do you know in which years the U.S. athletes won the most gold medals?

Swifter, Higher, Stronger

Superior athletes from around the world gather together to compete against each other as individuals. They also come as representatives of their countries. These men and women are Olympic athletes.

The Olympic Games have a history reaching back to ancient Greece. Many people think that the modern Olympics are the most exciting of sports spectacles. Athletes the world over devote their lives to training for the games. Like the early Greeks, these athletes have as their goal the motto *Citius, altius, fortius,* meaning "swifter, higher, stronger."

The oldest event in the Olympic Games is track and field. It was, and still is, the heart of the games. Even the Olympic motto is directed to the track-and-field athlete, for the Latin words encourage the athlete to run faster, jump higher, and throw harder.

The Beginning of the Olympics

The Olympics started in ancient Greece so long ago that their origin, or beginning, is not

> *The Olympics began when the Greek empire was at the height of its power.*

recorded by history. The ancient Greeks believed in excellence in every area of life. A Greek citizen was expected to have both a sound mind and a sound body. The Olympics were a celebration of the human body and what it could achieve.

The first Olympics recorded in history took place in 776 B.C.E. The Greeks have left us a picture of what the event was like. The games took place in the beautiful valley of Olympia. This was a sacred place where the Greeks came to worship their gods.

The grassy slopes of the valley served as a stadium for the games. In 776 B.C.E., over 45,000 Greeks watched and cheered the athletes competing in the games. The first person ever to have his name put in an Olympic record was Coroebus (kə REE bəs). Coroebus was a cook from the city of Elis (EE lis). He was the winner of a footrace of about 200 yards (180 meters).

✗ An Olympic winner became a great hero in ancient Greece. He was crowned with an olive wreath. The people of his city welcomed him

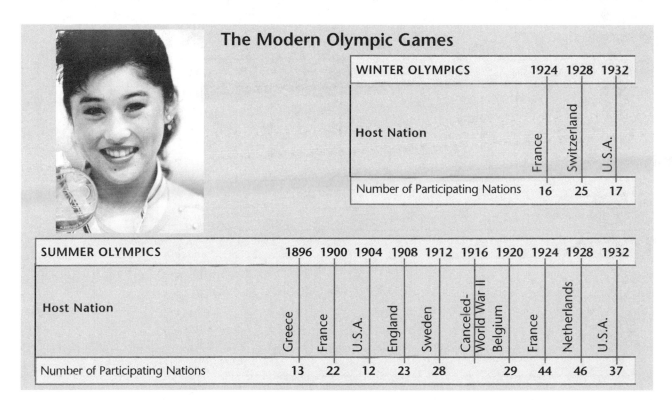

The Modern Olympic Games

WINTER OLYMPICS	1924	1928	1932
Host Nation	France	Switzerland	U.S.A.
Number of Participating Nations	16	25	17

SUMMER OLYMPICS	1896	1900	1904	1908	1912	1916	1920	1924	1928	1932
Host Nation	Greece	France	U.S.A.	England	Sweden	Canceled—World War II	Belgium	France	Netherlands	U.S.A.
Number of Participating Nations	13	22	12	23	28		29	44	46	37

home with parades. Poems were written about him, and statues were erected in his honor.

The physical strength and skill of the Greek athlete was so admired because the Greek nation was often at war. Warfare at the time meant hand-to-hand battle. Young Greek men had to be in good physical shape to be good soldiers. They might be called upon at any time to defend their country.

The Early Games

✔ In the first Olympic Games, there were only footraces. The <u>pentathlon</u> (pen TATH lon)—a contest consisting of five events—was later added to the games. The pentathlon tested an athlete in the long jump, javelin throw, footrace, discus throw, and wrestling. Wrestling soon became a favorite event in the games. Other events, including chariot racing—races between horse-drawn, two-wheel cars—came later.

One of the stories of outstanding Greek athletes is about the famed Milo (MY loh) of Croton (KROHT ən). He won the wrestling crown in six Games. He developed his great strength, it is said, by lifting a baby calf on his shoulder every day until it was a huge bull.

Another famous wrestler was Arrachion (ə RAK ee on) of Phigalia (fi GAYL ya). In one match, Arrachion was being strangled by an opponent. As he gasped for breath, Arrachion twisted his opponent's foot out of its socket. The opponent raised his hand to show he was defeated. Meanwhile, Arrachion died of strangulation. The Greeks crowned Arrachion's dead body with the winner's olive wreath.

The Olympics began when the Greek empire was at the height of its power. When Greece declined as a world power, the games lost their noble spirit. In 67 C.E., the Roman emperor Nero came to compete in the Olympic chariot races. Unjustly, he declared himself the winner.

The last of the early games was held about 390 C.E. Then, in 394 C.E., they were outlawed by the Christian emperor Theodosius I. After 1,200 years, the Olympics ended. During that long time, they had not been interrupted once, not even by war. And though the games were no longer played, their memory and spirit lived on.

The Modern Olympic Games

In 1896, the Olympics were reborn. For the first time in 1,506 years, an Olympic winner was crowned with an olive wreath. Once again, athletes met in competition.

The credit for the rebirth of the Olympics belongs to one person, the Baron de Courbertin of France. Courbertin believed that the Olympic games could serve the modern world as they had ancient Greece. The games would encourage physical fitness in young people. They would also promote world understanding and peace.

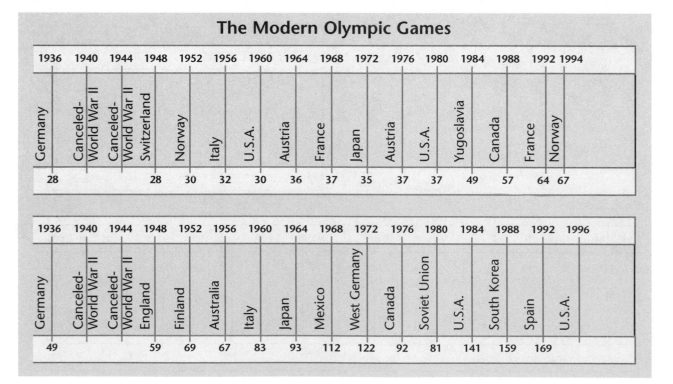

The Modern Olympic Games

1936	1940	1944	1948	1952	1956	1960	1964	1968	1972	1976	1980	1984	1988	1992	1994
Germany	Canceled-World War II	Canceled-World War II	Switzerland	Norway	Italy	U.S.A.	Austria	France	Japan	Austria	U.S.A.	Yugoslavia	Canada	France	Norway
28			28	30	32	30	36	37	35	37	37	49	57	64	67

1936	1940	1944	1948	1952	1956	1960	1964	1968	1972	1976	1980	1984	1988	1992	1996
Germany	Canceled-World War II	Canceled-World War II	England	Finland	Australia	Italy	Japan	Mexico	West Germany	Canada	Soviet Union	U.S.A.	South Korea	Spain	U.S.A.
49			59	69	67	83	93	112	122	92	81	141	159	169	

Alone, Courbertin began a campaign to revive, or bring back, the Olympics. Finally, in 1894, he gained support for his idea, and two years later, the first modern Olympic Games were held. Appropriately, the first modern Olympics took place in Athens, Greece. The games created excitement and enthusiasm throughout the world. At first, the United States as a nation did not support the Olympics. But after the 1896 games, the country caught Olympic fever. A major reason for the sudden interest in the Olympics was that the American athletes who competed in the track-and-field events in 1896 won nine out of the twelve events.

Many new games were included in the Olympics in 1896. The original track-and-field events were still the center of the games. But gymnastics, shooting, swimming, fencing, weight lifting, and other events were also added.

In 1912, the challenging decathlon—a track-and-field contest of ten events—was added to the Olympics. Athletes compete in this contest for two days. There are five events the first day. These include the 100-meter dash, long jump, shot put, high jump, and 400-meter run. Five more events follow on the second day. They are the 110-meter hurdles, discus throw, pole vault, javelin throw, and 1,500-meter run.

Over the years, the number of participants and the number of events in the games have grown. Women as well as men compete in today's Olympics. At their best, the Olympics reach the goal that the Baron de Courbertin had in mind when he revived them. In 1896, Courbertin wrote these words about the games: "The important thing in the Olympic Games is not to win, but to take part, just as the important thing in life is not the triumph but the struggle; the essential thing is not to have conquered but to have fought well."

RECALLING FACTS

1. Number the following events in the order in which they happened.

   _____ The emperor Nero won an Olympic chariot race.

   _____ Coroebus set an Olympic footracing record.

   _____ The first modern Olympic Games were held in Athens, Greece.

   _____ The emperor Theodosius outlawed the Olympics.

   _____ Wrestling was added to the games.

2. What effect did the decline of the Greek empire have on the early Olympic Games?

   _____

   _____

3. Where were the early Olympics and the first modern Olympics both held?

   _____

4. What new events were added to the Olympics in 1896?

   _____

   _____

5. Why did the Baron de Courbertin revive the Olympics?

   _____

   _____

   _____

   _____

   _____

6. Match the events in the right column with the dates in the left column.

   _____ 776 B.C.E.   a. beginning of the modern Olympics

   _____ 390 C.E.   b. first Olympic Games ever recorded

   _____ 1896 C.E.   c. last recorded early Olympic Games

7. Reread the paragraph in the selection marked with an X. Underline its main idea. Then circle two or more details that support the main idea.

8. Draw a line to match each word with its meaning.

revive   a contest of five events

decathlon   to bring back or make popular

pentathlon   a contest of ten events

INTERPRETING FACTS

1. Write the cause for the effect described below.

   Cause _____

   _____

   Effect Many of the early Olympic events tested physical skills needed by Greek soldiers.

2. The ancient Greeks believed in both a sound body and a sound mind. Compare their belief about this with the feelings of Americans today.

   _____

   _____

   _____

   _____

   _____

   _____

3. During what span of time were the Olympic Games not held?

   _____

   _____

4. Why did the events in the Olympics change over the years?

   _____

   _____

5. Reread the paragraph in the selection that has a check mark next to it. Write a sentence that expresses the main idea.

   _____

   _____

6. Do you think the Baron de Courbertin's statement about the Olympics on page 135 is still true about the Olympics today? Explain.

   _____

   _____

7. a. Is the Baron de Courbertin's statement a fact or an opinion?

   _____

   b. In two sentences, tell why you agree or disagree with the statement.

   _____

   _____

   _____

8. Do you think the Olympic motto "Swifter, higher, stronger" is still appropriate? Explain.

   _____

   _____

   _____

9. Explain how the Olympic Games have always been democratic in spirit.

_____

_____

_____

_____

10. Why might the decathlon be considered the supreme Olympic event?

_____

_____

_____

_____

SKILL FOCUS

Use the timeline on pages 133 and 134 to answer the following questions.

1. How frequently are the Olympic Games held? _____

2. In what year did the greatest number of nations participate in the games? _____

3. a. In what years were the Olympic Games canceled?

   _____   _____   _____

   b. Why were the games canceled? _____

   _____

   _____

4. Where were the summer and winter Olympics held in the first games after World War II?

   _____

5. Where and when were the first winter Olympic Games held? _____

6. In what year were both the summer and the winter games held in Germany? _____

7. As of 1994, how many games, summer and winter, had been held in the United States?

   _____

8. In which two countries have the most Olympic Games been held? _____

9. Look at the number of nations participating in the summer Olympics. What trend do you

   see from 1896 to 1994? _____

   _____

10. Have the winter Olympics ever been held in Greece? _____ In one sentence,

   explain why this might be so. _____

   _____

▶ **Real Life Connections** What sport would you like to see as a new Olympic event? Give your reasons.

Following Directions

___ Reading a Science Selection ___

▶ **Background Information**

Following directions is an important skill. You will need to follow directions countless times in your life.

In the following selection, you will be asked to follow directions to carry out a scientific experiment. The selection has five sections. The first two describe the scientific meaning of work and the different forces that are involved. Read these sections carefully and study the diagrams. Be sure that you understand each of the boldfaced terms and equations.

The third and fourth sections describe how two simple machines—levers and pulleys—make work easier. While you read these sections, review the equations in the first part of the selection.

▶ **Skill Focus**

Following directions is an important skill. For example, to carry out an experiment in a science textbook, you must follow directions.

Directions for an experiment are set up in a certain way. Most sets of directions have five parts: Problem, Aim, Materials,

Procedure, and Observations or Conclusions. Like recipes, science experiments are always set up the same way so that they can be repeated any number of times exactly as they were done the first time. The following describes each part.

Problem: The question that you should be able to answer at the end of the experiment

Aim: What will be done in the experiment

Materials: Equipment or objects needed for the experiment

Procedure: The steps that must be carried out in order to complete the experiment

Observations or Conclusions: Questions to answer or conclusions to draw about the outcome of the experiment

Use the following steps to read a science selection with directions for an experiment.

1. Read the paragraphs that explain the ideas. Be sure that you understand the ideas.

2. Read through the five parts of the directions: Problem, Aim, Materials, Procedure, and Observations or Conclusions. Be sure that you understand all the scientific words.

3. Study the pictures or

diagrams. Be sure to read the captions and labels.

4. Reread the Problem, Aim, Materials, Procedure, and Observations or Conclusions. Be sure that you understand the procedure before you begin the experiment.

▶ **Word Clues**

Sometimes special terms are explained in a paragraph and also shown in a diagram. When this happens, study both the text and the diagram to understand the terms.

Use **diagram** clues and context clues to find out the meaning of the three underlined terms in the selection.

▶ **Strategy Tip**

After you have read and understood the sections on levers and pulleys in "Work and Machines," study the directions for the experiment on page 140. Use the four steps to help you. Following directions in this way can be very useful to you.

WORK AND MACHINES

People use machines every day. Some machines are complicated and have many moving parts. Others are so simple that most people don't think of them as machines. A machine is any invention that makes work easier or faster.

What Is Work?

To a scientist, work has a special meaning. Work means the use of force to move an object through a distance. The object is moved in the direction of the force. This meaning for work can be expressed in an equation.

$$\text{Work} = \text{Force} \times \text{Distance}$$

To move an object, a machine must overcome the force that resists the movement of the object. This force is the **resistance.** The distance through which the machine moves the object is called the **resistance distance.**

How Do Machines Make Work Easier?

When a machine is used, some work goes into making the machine function. The force applied by the user to a machine is called the **effort.** The distance through which the user applies the effort is called the **effort distance.** Some machines make work easier by increasing the amount of force that is applied to them and using it against the resistance force. The amount by which a machine increases a force is called the **mechanical advantage** of the machine.

$$\text{Mechanical Advantage} = \text{Resistance} \div \text{Effort}$$

Figure 1. A lever is a simple machine made up of a rigid arm that pivots on a point called a fulcrum.

Figure 2. A lever makes moving a heavy object easier by applying force through a greater distance.

Levers

A **lever** is a simple machine that can multiply a small effort force to overcome a large resistance force. A lever is like a seesaw. It has a rigid arm that rocks back and forth on a fixed point called the fulcrum. The woman in Figure 1 is using a simple lever. What is the resistance? How is the effort being applied?

The rigid arm of every lever has two parts. The effort arm is the distance between the fulcrum and the effort force. The resistance arm is the distance between the fulcrum and the resistance force. You can figure out the mechanical advantage of a lever by dividing the length of the effort arm by the length of the resistance arm.

$$\text{Mechanical Advantage} = \text{Effort Arm} \div \text{Resistance Arm}$$

In Figure 2, the resistance arm is 1 meter, and the effort arm is 5 meters. The mechanical advantage of this lever, then, is 5. On a seesaw, the effort arm and the resistance arm are equal. Therefore, the mechanical advantage of a seesaw is 1.

You can figure out how much effort is needed to move an object if you know the mechanical advantage of a machine. To do this, you divide the resistance by the mechanical advantage.

$$\text{Effort} = \text{Resistance} \div \text{Mechanical Advantage}$$

Pulleys

A **pulley,** another highly useful simple machine, is a form of lever. A pulley makes work easier by changing the direction of a

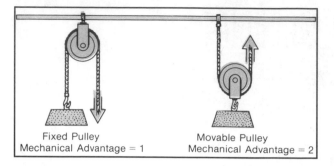

Fixed Pulley
Mechanical Advantage = 1

Movable Pulley
Mechanical Advantage = 2

Figure 3. A fixed pulley, at left, is held in place by a support beam. At right, a movable pulley moves freely on a rope attached to a support beam.

force. A pulley is a grooved wheel over which runs a cord. To lift an object with a pulley, you pull on the cord. Your pull is the effort. The object that is pulled is the resistance.

A pulley attached to a wall, a beam, or any other support frame is called a **fixed pulley.** Window shades and flagpoles often have fixed pulleys. Fixed pulleys do not multiply the effort force put into them. They only change the direction of the force. Often it is easier to pull against a resistance than to lift it.

A greater advantage is gained through using a **movable pulley.** A movable pulley is hung on a rope attached to a support frame. The rope runs through the pulley. The pulley itself moves up the rope as the rope is pulled. A movable pulley makes it easier to lift a heavy weight. You can figure out the mechanical advantage of a pulley by dividing the resistance distance by the effort distance.

Mechanical Advantage =
Resistance Distance ÷ Effort Distance

Experiment

The following experiment will show the advantage of a fixed pulley.

Problem

What mechanical advantage can you obtain by using a pulley?

Aim

In this experiment, you will measure the mechanical advantage of a fixed pulley.

Materials

You will need a support frame, a single lightweight pulley, a length of cord, a kilogram weight, a spring balance, and a meter stick.

Procedure

1. Attach the weight to the spring balance. What is the weight of the load, or the resistance?

2. Remove the weight from the spring balance. Tie the weight to one end of the cord. String the free end of the cord over the pulley. Hang the pulley on the support frame and attach the top of the spring balance to the free end of the cord. Pull slowly on the spring balance. Read the spring balance to determine the value of this effort. How does the effort compare to the resistance? Was it easier to lift the weight by hand or to lift it with the use of the pulley? Why?

3. Use the meter stick to see how far you must pull down the cord to lift the weight 1 meter. Then compare the two distances. What is the mechanical advantage of a fixed pulley?

Observations or Conclusions

The mechanical advantage of a fixed pulley is 1. Think about what this means. Why is a fixed pulley useful?

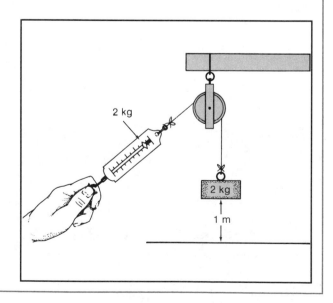

RECALLING FACTS

1. What is a machine? _____

_____

2. What is the mechanical advantage of a machine?

_____

3. In Figure 1, what is the fulcrum?

_____

4. Draw a line to match each term with its explanation.

fulcrum   distance between the fulcrum and the effort force

effort arm   distance between the fulcrum and the resistance force

resistance arm   fixed point over which a lever rocks

INTERPRETING FACTS

1. If a lever has an effort arm of 4 meters and a resistance arm of 2 meters, what is the mechanical advantage of the

machine? _____

2. Which tool is not a lever: a pair of scissors, a nutcracker, a crowbar, an axe?

_____

3. A pair of scissors is a kind of lever. Where is the fulcrum on a pair of scissors?

_____

4. On a pair of scissors, where is the effort applied? What provides the resistance?

_____

5. How far must you raise the cord of a movable pulley in order to lift a load 2

meters? _____

6. How could you make a seesaw work better as a lever?

_____

_____

SKILL FOCUS

Write a summary of the experiment on page 140 in your own words. Do not look back. Then check your summary by rereading the experiment. Make any necessary corrections.

_____

_____

_____

_____

The following experiment should show how much force it would take to lift an object of a certain weight with two different levers. Complete the directions using the experiment on page 140 as a model. Use a ruler or a metric stick for the arm. Use a block of wood for the fulcrum. Use a weight for the resistance. Use other weights to measure the effort needed to lift the resistance. A spring balance will be necessary for this experiment. Be sure to number the steps in the Procedure part. In the box, draw and label a diagram to show what is to be done. The Problem and Aim have been completed for you.

Experiment

Problem

Compare the effort needed to lift an object of a certain weight with two different levers.

Aim

In this experiment, you will compare the effort force needed to lift a resistance of a certain weight with two different levers. The effort arm of one lever should be twice the length of the resistance arm. The effort arm of the other lever should be four times the length of the resistance arm.

Materials

_____

_____

_____

_____

Procedure

_____

_____

_____

_____

_____

_____

_____

_____

_____

_____

_____

Observations and Conclusions

_____

_____

▶ **Real Life Connections** Name a kind of pulley and a kind of lever that you use daily.

Circle Graphs

Reading a Mathematics Selection

▶ Background Information

Reading graphs is an important skill to learn. You will find graphs in newspapers and magazines. Graphs often appear in news stories. Facts about an opinion poll on a topic, for example, will often show you the result in a circle graph. This type of graph lets you see at a glance the percentage of people who approve, disapprove, or have no opinion on this topic.

If you are interested in the performance of a team over a period of several months or years, then you may find information about this subject shown in a bar graph. The different heights of the bars enable you to compare the high points and low points in the performance of the team from month to month or from year to year.

When changes over time are smaller and more numerous, a line graph probably will be used to show them. For example. suppose that you want to know the rise and fall of the cost of living week by week over a period of two months. A line graph would show this

information. Looking at this graph, you would get a clearer picture of changes in the cost of living during the two-month period.

▶ Skill Focus

Graphs show information very clearly. You can read a graph much more quickly than you can read a paragraph that gives the same information. Graphs also make it easier for you to compare information.

Different graphs are used for different purposes. **Circle graphs** are used for showing parts of a whole. Circle graphs are usually used with percents.

When you look at a circle graph, it may be helpful to think of it as a pizza. The next time you eat a pizza, think about how each slice fits into the whole. For example if the pizza is evenly divided into 8 slices and you eat 2 slices, you have eaten 2/8 of the pie, which is 1/4 of it. As a percent, 1/4 is 25%.

Notice that you are dealing with a percentage or a part of a whole. The pizza, or the circle, represents the whole. The bigger the segment is, the bigger the percentage will be. Circle graphs are easy

to understand. If you understand what these graphs are representing, then you will find circle graphs very useful for getting information quickly.

However, before you can understand the facts in a graph, you need to know the purpose of the graph. Be sure to read the paragraphs that come before a graph and the title of the graph. Then you will be able to use the information that the graph presents in a variety of ways.

▶ Word Clues

When you read "Reading Graphs," look for these important words: *data, sectors,* and *label.* They will help you understand more about circle graphs.

▶ Strategy Tip

Be sure to read the title of each graph before you study the graph itself. Also, take the time to understand what the labels stand for. Only by doing these things will you be able to understand details on a graph accurately.

Reading Graphs

**Total Medals,
1994 Winter Olympics**

*Switzerland, Austria, S. Korea, Finland

**Gold Medals,
1994 Winter Olympics**

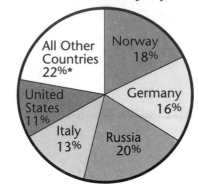

*Canada, Switzerland, Austria, S. Korea, Finland

The graph above is a **circle graph**. The first thing that you should read is the title of the graph. The title tells what kind of information is shown in the graph. The title of this graph is *Total Medals, 1994 Winter Olympics*.

This circle graph is divided into seven sections that show **data,** or information. The sections are called **sectors.** Each sector has a label. The label tells you what the sector stands for. When you read a circle graph, the sectors help you compare data. For example, in this circle graph, the sectors help you compare the total number of medals won by countries in the 1994 Winter Olympics. By looking at the size of the sectors, you can see that Norway won the most medals of the six countries named on the graph. The United States and Canada won the fewest medals. The note below the graph tells you that there were four other countries that won medals—Switzerland, Austria, South Korea, and Finland. The size of the sectors also tells you that four-fifths of the medals were won by Norway, Germany, Russia, Italy, the United States, and Canada. All the other countries won one-fifth of the medals.

There is another circle graph next to the first one. The title tells you that this graph can help you compare gold medals won in the 1994 Winter Olympics. The sectors are labeled with the names of the countries and percents. The graph shows that Russia won the greatest number of gold medals. The United States won the fewest number of gold medals.

When percents are shown on a circle graph,

they should always add up to 100, which stands for the whole circle. The percents make it easier to compare information. In the graph above, you can see that Russia won one-fifth of the gold medals. Because percents are shown, you can also see that Russia won 9 percent more medals than the United States.

The circle graph below can help you

**Silver Medals,
1994 Winter Olympics**

*Switzerland, Austria, S. Korea, Finland

compare the number of silver medals won in the 1994 Winter Olympics. Each sector in this circle graph is also labeled with a percent. Norway won the most silver medals, with 21 percent. The United States won 10 percent of the medals.

This circle graph shows a great deal of data, but it does not show how many medals were won by each group of countries. You know that the United States won about 10 percent of the silver medals. If the total number of medals were given, you could solve the following numerical sentence:

$$10\% \text{ of } t = m, \text{ or } \frac{10}{100} \times t = m$$

The symbol t stands for the total number of medals won. The symbol m stands for the number of medals won by the United States.

There were a total of 51 silver medals won in the 1994 Winter Olympics. Now you can solve the sentence.

$$\frac{10}{100} \times 51 = m, \text{ or } \frac{10}{100} \times \frac{51}{1} = m$$

$$\frac{510}{100} = m, \text{ or } \frac{510}{100} = 5.1$$

The figure of 5.1 is not an exact number because sometimes percents on circle graphs are rounded off. If you round off the number 5.1, you will find that the United States won five medals in the 1994 Winter Olympics.

When sectors in a circle graph are labeled and the percents are not given, you can still compare the size of the sectors. You can tell which is greatest, which is least, and which are about the same. You can also estimate the amount using fractions.

When the sectors are labeled with percents, you can find how much larger one sector is than another. Also, if the total amount is given as data, you can multiply to find the amount in each sector.

RECALLING FACTS

1. What does the title of a graph tell?

_____

2. What use can be made of the total amount when it is given as data?

_____

_____

3. How many sectors are shown in the last circle graph in the selection?

_____

_____

4. In the graph about 1994 Silver Medal Winners, Canada, Norway, and Germany won a total of 47% of the medals. What percent did all the other nations included win?

_____

5. Using the first circle graph in the selection, what is the percent of medals won by Norway, Germany, Russia, Italy, the United States, and Canada combined, if all the other countries won 20 percent?

_____

INTERPRETING FACTS

1. Why are circle graphs useful for showing percents? _____

2. What determines the size of a sector in a circle graph?_____

3. If the size of one sector of a circle graph were increased, what would happen to the other sectors?

_____

4. Put a check mark next to the idea that could best be shown in a circle graph.

_____ increase in attendance at Olympic games from 1896 to 1994

_____ countries winning medals in speed skating in the 1994 Winter Olympics

_____ winning times for women's downhill skiing in the 1994 Winter Olympics

A. Use the graphs in the selection to answer the following questions.

1. Which country won the greatest number of medals overall in the 1994 Winter Olympics?

_____

2. What is the title of the second graph?

_____

_____

3. Which two countries won the same total number of medals in the 1994 Winter Olympics?

_____

4. Which country won 16% of the silver medals in the 1994 Winter Olympics?

_____

B. Use the graph below to answer the questions that follow.

Medals Won by Italy, 1994 Winter Olympics

Bronze Medals 40%

Gold Medals 35%

Silver Medals 25%

Total number of medals won in all: 20.

1. What is the title of the graph?

_____

_____

2. How many sectors are shown?

_____

3. How are the sectors labeled?

_____

_____

4. What is the sum of the percents?

_____

5. What are the three types of medals that Italy won in the 1994 Winter Olympics?

_____

6. Of the three types of medals, which type did Italy win most?

_____

7. Of the three types of medals, which type did Italy win the fewest of?

_____

8. What percent of the medals won by Italy were gold medals?

_____

9. How many gold medals did Italy win?

_____

10. How many silver medals did Italy win?

_____

11. How many bronze medals did Italy win?

_____

▶ **Real Life Connections** Research facts about your community. Put the information into a circle graph.

Lesson 45

Multiple Meanings

A word may have a different meaning in literature, social studies, science, mathematics, or music. Some words with multiple meanings follow.

| band | change | crop | legend | pupil | yard |
| cell | cone | front | power | scale | plot |

Read the two definitions for each word below. Choose a word from the list above that fits those two definitions. Write the word on the line above the definitions.

1. _____

   Mathematics: a measure, 36 inches in length

   Social Studies: an open place used for a business or special purpose

2. _____

   Music: a group of musicians playing instruments together

   Social Studies: a group of people joined to do something

3. _____

   Social Studies: a small room in a prison or jail

   Science: the basic unit of living matter, usually very small

4. _____

   Mathematics: a solid object that narrows evenly from a flat circle at one end to a point at the other

   Science: the part of evergreen trees that bears seeds

5. _____

   Mathematics: money returned when one has paid more than the amount owed

   Social Studies: places or conditions that become different as time passes

6. _____

   Literature: the action, or series of events, in a story

   Social Studies: a secret plan, in politics or during a war, to gain power or harm an enemy, by misleading people, usually by dishonest methods

7. _____

   Science: energy or force that has the ability to do work

   Social Studies: a person or group that has authority, right, or control over others

8. _____

   Science: the dark opening in the center of the eye

   Social Studies: a person being taught by a teacher

9. _____

   Social Studies: the full amount of produce grown by a farmer in one season

   Science: a pouch in a bird's gullet where food is softened for digestion

10. _____

   Literature: a story handed down through the years and connected with some real events, but probably not true in itself

   Social Studies: a title or description under a picture or map

11. _____

   Science: the boundary between two large masses of air

   Social Studies: in a war, the part where the fighting is going on

12. _____

   Music: a series of musical tones arranged in order from lowest to highest or highest to lowest

   Science: any of the thin, flat, hard plates that cover and protect certain fish

Using an Index

The quickest way to find information in a text or reference book is to use the **index.** An index lists all the important subjects included in the book.

On the following page is part of an index from a science textbook. The **topics** are arranged in alphabetical order. Find the topic *Oil*. Below it, three subtopics are listed alphabetically: *pollution from, source,* and *use.* **Subtopics** list the specific kinds of information given in the book about the topic. Notice that some subtopics have such words as *in* and *of* before them. As you can see, these short words don't affect the alphabetical order of the subtopics.

The numbers after each topic or subtopic are the page numbers on which information is found. Numbers separated by dashes indicate that information begins on the page before the dash and ends on the page after the dash. Numbers separated by commas show that information appears on only the pages for which numbers are given.

Study the index on the following page. Then answer the questions on the lines provided.

1. On what page(s) would you find information about mud? _____

2. How many subtopics are listed under the topic *Moon*? _____

3. On what page(s) would you find information about craters on the moon? _____

4. How many pages does the book have on nuclear energy? _____

5. On what page(s) would you find information about the moons of Pluto? _____

6. How many pages does the book have on the Milky Way? _____

7. On what page(s) would you find information about nitrogen in the soil? _____

8. What two planets' moons are discussed on the same page? _____.

9. If you wanted information on life in the oceans, which page would you *not* read between pages 250 and 256? _____

10. On what page(s) would you find information about nickel in the earth's core? _____

11. What five subtopics about the moon are discussed on page 105?

_____

12. What topic comes between nickel and nuclear energy? _____

13. If the book had information about mold, after which topic would it be listed? _____

14. If the book had information about fish farms in the oceans, before which subtopic would it be listed? _____

Methane, 475
    in atmosphere, 262
    in outer planets, 75, 77
Milky Way, 25–28, 38–41, 47, 57
Minerals:
    chemical weathering of, 320–324
    conservation of, 473–474
    crystals, 138–140, 161–162
    deposits, 171–172
    gems, 143–145
    identification of, 138, 145–153
    in lithosphere, 29
    in rocks, 158, 161, 168, 323
    soil and, 324–327, 330
    sources of, 141–142, 470–472, 489
Mining, 471–474
Moho, 187, 188
Mohs scale, 148–149
Molecules, behavior of, 122–124, 125
Moon:
    age of, 103, 444–446
    atmosphere of, 104
    axis, rotation of, 102–103
    craters on, 79, 104–105
    eclipses, 108–109
    gravity of, 102
    marias, 103–104, 105
    orbit of, 105
    phases, 105–107, 108
    revolution of, 105
    size, 102
    tides and, 109–111
Moons:
    of Jupiter, 75
    of Mars, 74
    of Neptune, 77
    of Pluto, 78
    of Saturn, 76
    of Uranus, 77
Moraines, 345–346
Mountains, 200–202, 452, 454
    belts, 202
    earth's mantle and, 367–368
    erosion and, 30, 201
    faults and, 372
    folds and, 375, 376
    magma and, 377
    oceanic, 240, 248–250, 404–406
    ores in, 333
    ranges, 201–202, 402–403, 411,
        453, 456
    soils, 332–333
    system of, 202
    weathering and, 30
Mud, 165

N

Nebulae, 40
Nekton, 251, 252, 253
Neon:
    in atmosphere, 94
    in meteoroids, 81
Nickel:
    in the earth's core, 192–193
    in meteoroids, 81
Nitrogen:
    in atmosphere, 30, 94, 263–265,
        275
    from carbon, 14, 443
    living things and, 264–265,
        481–482
    in oceans, 242
    in soil, 324, 469
Nuclear energy, 492–494
Nucleus, 127

O

Oceans:
    basins, topography of, 244–250,
        255, 257
    continental margins, 245–246
    depths, 238, 241, 243, 245–246,
        250, 251, 252, 253–254
    gases in, 242
    life in, 250–254, 256, 426
    minerals in, 490
    oceanography, 13, 239, 241,
        254–257
    salinity, 239–242, 251, 256
    spreading of floor, 404–407, 454
    temperatures and, 241, 242–243,
        256, 309
    trenches, 249, 406–407
Oil:
    pollution from, 482–483
    source, 474, 475
    use, 324, 476
Orbit, 24, 69
    of planets, 68–69, 70–76
    of satellites, 87–89
Orbital velocity, 87–89
Ores, 141–142, 143, 333, 470–471
    mining, 471–472
    refining, 472–473
Oxidation, 320–321

Comparing Travel Packages

In planning a vacation, you need to decide on many things—where you will go, how long you will stay, what hotel you will stay at, what you want to see, and how much money you will spend. **Travel packages** are arrangements made by a travel agent or travel company to cover your vacation plans. These arrangements may include any of the following: air travel, hotels, meals, and such extras as sightseeing. Before making a decision on your travel plans, look into several travel packages to compare what they offer.

Carefully read and compare the following travel packages.

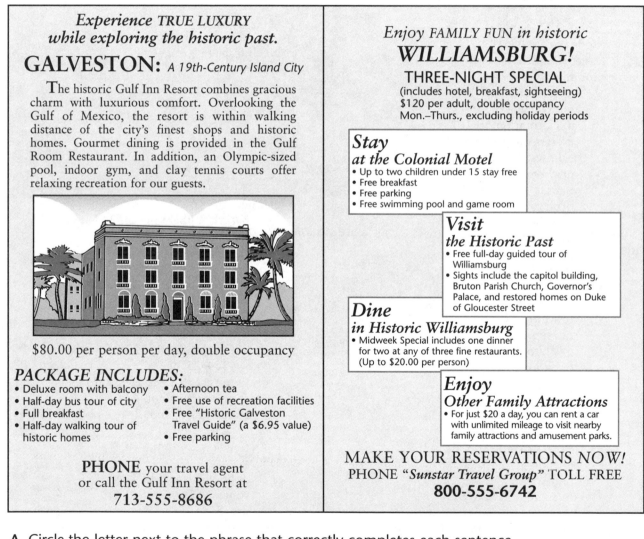

Experience TRUE LUXURY *while exploring the historic past.*

GALVESTON: *A 19th-Century Island City*

The historic Gulf Inn Resort combines gracious charm with luxurious comfort. Overlooking the Gulf of Mexico, the resort is within walking distance of the city's finest shops and historic homes. Gourmet dining is provided in the Gulf Room Restaurant. In addition, an Olympic-sized pool, indoor gym, and clay tennis courts offer relaxing recreation for our guests.

$80.00 per person per day, double occupancy

PACKAGE INCLUDES:
- Deluxe room with balcony
- Half-day bus tour of city
- Full breakfast
- Half-day walking tour of historic homes
- Afternoon tea
- Free use of recreation facilities
- Free "Historic Galveston Travel Guide" (a $6.95 value)
- Free parking

PHONE your travel agent or call the Gulf Inn Resort at
713-555-8686

Enjoy FAMILY FUN *in historic*

WILLIAMSBURG!
THREE-NIGHT SPECIAL
(includes hotel, breakfast, sightseeing)
$120 per adult, double occupancy
Mon.–Thurs., excluding holiday periods

Stay at the Colonial Motel
- Up to two children under 15 stay free
- Free breakfast
- Free parking
- Free swimming pool and game room

Visit the Historic Past
- Free full-day guided tour of Williamsburg
- Sights include the capitol building, Bruton Parish Church, Governor's Palace, and restored homes on Duke of Gloucester Street

Dine in Historic Williamsburg
- Midweek Special includes one dinner for two at any of three fine restaurants. (Up to $20.00 per person)

Enjoy Other Family Attractions
- For just $20 a day, you can rent a car with unlimited mileage to visit nearby family attractions and amusement parks.

MAKE YOUR RESERVATIONS NOW!
PHONE *"Sunstar Travel Group"* TOLL FREE
800-555-6742

A. Circle the letter next to the phrase that correctly completes each sentence.

1. The Galveston package stresses
    a. family fun.   **b.** sightseeing.   **c.** luxury accommodations.

2. The Williamsburg package stresses
    a. family fun.   **b.** sightseeing.   **c.** luxury accommodations.

3. The rates for both packages are based on "double occupancy," which means that
    a. the charge is the same for two people in the room as it is for one person.
    b. the per-person charge is based on two people in a room, so the price is twice the quoted rate.
    c. the room rate changes with each additional person in the room.

4. If a family wants to save money, it may prefer the Williamsburg package because
    a. up to two children can stay free in the motel.
    b. the package offers a free dinner for two.
    c. the package offers use of a pool and game room at the motel.

5. For three nights, the Galveston package costs
    a. $240.00 per person.   b. $240.00 per room.   c. $80.00 per person.

6. Staying in Williamsburg for three nights will cost more than the advertised package price because the package
    a. does not include any sightseeing tours.
    b. does not include any dinners.
    c. includes breakfasts and one dinner for two, so additional meals will be extra.

7. Both the Galveston and Williamsburg packages include
    a. a special three-day rate for rooms.
    b. a room rate based upon double occupancy.
    c. nightly room rates.

B. Compare the two travel packages by completing the chart below. If no information is given for a particular item, write *no information*. Then answer the questions below the chart.

	GALVESTON	WILLIAMSBURG
price per night per adult		
number of people per room		
days available		
children's rates		
meals included		
free recreation facilities		
number of tours		
car rental		
how to reserve		

1. Which package is less expensive per night? _____

2. Which package includes more free recreation facilities? _____

3. Which package allows more people in one room? _____

4. Which package provides more free meals? _____

5. Which package is available on weekends? _____

Lesson 48 _____

Point of View

Reading a Literature Selection _____

▶ Background Information

Computers continue to change the way people live, work, and think. This story, in the form of a journal, is about a computer named Dellie, described in the day-to-day journal entries of a student.

▶ Skill Focus

Before writing, an author must decide whether the story will be told by one of the characters or by an outsider. The **point of view** determines the kind of information that is given in a story and how it is presented.

When the events of the story are seen through the eyes of a character who participated in the events, the author is using **first-person point of view**. The narrator tells the reader his or her thoughts. The narrator cannot enter the minds of the other characters. Thus, the narrator tells only what he or she actually *sees* others doing.

Read the following paragraph.

Walking home, I heard someone running toward me. I was frightened. A tall man ran by me. He raced to an emergency police phone. He spoke loudly and asked for an ambulance. Feeling relieved, I asked if I could be of any help.

This event is seen through the eyes of a narrator. The reader learns only what the narrator thinks and feels, not how the other character feels or what he or she is thinking.

When you try to determine the point of view, think about the following questions.
1. Is the narrator a participant in the event or an outsider?
2. Do you know what only the narrator is thinking and feeling?
3. Do you know what the other characters are thinking and feeling?

▶ Word Clues

When you read a word that you don't know, look for context clues to understand it. Sometimes, however, there may be no context clues. Read the sentence below.

Technicians have been trying to put together the six computer pieces so that our new principal can start functioning properly.

Suppose that you do not know the meaning of the word *technicians*. There are no context clues. You will have to look up the word in a dictionary. You may find it convenient to finish reading first and then look up the word.

Use a **dictionary** to find the meaning of the three underlined words in the selection.

▶ Strategy Tip

"The Principal Problem" is written from the first-person point of view. As you read it, notice that the information is limited to the narrator's own thoughts and feelings. Recognizing the point of view will give you a better understanding of a story's characters and plot.

The Principal Problem

September 10 It had to happen, of course. Vacation's come to an end—summer, too, for that matter—and today, I, Carmen Soares, began my last year at Gloria Willis Junior High. I wish it were my last week, though I'm relieved to have Miss James for my homeroom teacher. She's got potential; she just has to be trained right. Seat assignments were handed out, and I'm right in front of Harry Seely. How's that for luck? He asked to borrow a pencil, and I very coolly said, "Keep it, Harry; I've got zillions of them." Definitely a good start!

September 11 A weird thing happened at our first assembly of the year. Mr. Alioto, the assistant principal, announced that Mrs. Uxley would not be returning as principal of Gloria Willis. I guess she's retiring or something. When one of the kids asked about Mrs. Uxley's replacement, Mr. Alioto didn't say anything for a moment, then answered, "Her replacement will be delivered next week."

September 14 I've done nothing for the last three days but wonder about our new principal. How do you "deliver" a principal?

September 19 Well, I got my answer today—you deliver a principal in boxes. Our principal was delivered in six boxes, to be exact. It's a computer—talk about new ideas! It's a good thing that I'm heading for high school after this year. But Luis Garcia says that won't make a bit of difference. He told me that once they get a bad idea in one school, they usually take it around to all the others.

September 23 Technicians have been trying to put together the six computer pieces so that our new principal can start functioning properly. They've been running in and out of the principal's office. Rumors are racing around the school, but no one really knows what's happening. Harry Seely borrowed another pencil. That makes three. What does he do with them?

September 24 Two items of interest! First, they put a suggestion box in each classroom; then they gave everyone, even teachers, a form to complete. In the top part, you had to write your hobbies, your favorite television shows, even the kinds of food that you like best. Also, they wanted you to suggest how life at Gloria Willis could be improved. They also handed out this funny note:

> HELLO:
>   MY NAME IS T12H2679DELTA. CALL ME DELLIE. I AM YOUR NEW PRINCIPAL. ALL NEW DELTA COMPUTERS ARE PROGRAMMED FOR TOP PERFORMANCE IN A SPECIFIC TYPE OF JOB, AND I AM NO EXCEPTION. A SUGGESTION BOX HAS BEEN PLACED IN YOUR CLASSROOM. PLEASE USE IT OFTEN SO THAT YOU CAN HELP ME IN MY JOB. I THINK WE CAN HAVE FUN TOGETHER, DON'T YOU?

September 26 As if things weren't bad enough, I came across a magazine article about my new principal. It said that there were two Delta computers now in use: ours, and one that's working as a town manager out in some small midwestern town. The article talked about how the other Delta has to be a diplomat, which means it has to consider everybody's opinion before it makes any decisions. Our Delta principal, on the other hand, is supposed to act like a dictator. It makes decisions without considering anyone's opinion. I think we're in big, big trouble at Gloria Willis—really gigantic trouble!

September 27 I detest Harry Seely—he's been borrowing Rita Korngold's pencils, too.

September 28 All's well that ends well. Rita Korngold was shipped off to the other side of the room. I don't think it had anything to do with my suggestion, although it was really a very funny <u>coincidence</u>. I dropped another suggestion into the box just to be sure.

September 29 That'll teach me. I thought I was safe telling Milos Kelly, the track star, about the suggestion box, but that just shows how smart I really am! When Miss James said gym was being replaced by <u>aerobics</u>, I knew whose suggestion that was. I just hope she keeps her promise not to tell anyone else.

October 2 Now I know what Milos Kelly's promises are worth! When I walked into class this morning, there was a long line of kids waiting to drop suggestions into the box. To make things worse, when I went to my seat, I found out that Harry Seely was no longer sitting in back of me. He'd been moved to the other side of the room, to a seat next to—Guess Who? They put Ronnie Franks behind me in Harry Seely's place. What a trade that was! Now I'll have to stop wearing my hair in a braid. Ronnie Franks is that kind of neighbor. After I finish writing this, I'm going to spend at least two hours writing suggestions.

October 3 Things are getting weird, to say the least. There's a ten-minute wait at just about every suggestion box in school— at any time of day! Mr. Alioto must have announced six different big changes in school policy over the public address system today. Twice he changed a policy that had been set only yesterday. I wonder who suggested that we be allowed to bring our pets to school.

> *It seems the people in that town are having a lot of trouble with their computer.*

October 5 War was declared in school today, and it's our class against 9C. They started it. Just after we sat down in the auditorium, Mr. Alioto said, "It's been suggested that some of the classes change places at assembly." He said "some of the classes," but he changed only two. Guess which two? What hurt was the way 9C carried on as we walked to the rear of the auditorium.

October 6 Every kid in class suggested that we change assembly places again. Later, during hide and seek, Mr. Alioto announced that there wouldn't be homework anymore. Everybody shouted and clapped, but I felt kind of sad. I wonder what's wrong with me?

October 7 I told my mother that I wanted to move to a new school. When she asked me why, I didn't know what to say. How could I explain that I was tired of seeing movies and playing games all day? She'd take me to a doctor; I'm sure she would.

October 8 I spent most of the day in the nurse's office. Cindy Marshall's snake bit me. Looking over the magazines that they have at the nurse's office now, I came across a story about that Delta computer that's running a town out in the Midwest. It seems the people in that town are having a lot of trouble with their computer. It makes them stand in lines according to their height and gives out demerits when they are late. In a way, I wish that our principal was more like the town manager.

October 13 A quiet day. Our clown phoned in sick, and the movie projector exploded. I dropped six suggestions into the box suggesting that we be allowed to do plain old schoolwork again. No one can ever know about those suggestions! We still didn't get our old seats back in assembly.

October 14 Miss James told us there would be an election in school next month. When we asked her what the election was for, she became very upset. Ronnie Franks tapped me on the shoulder and threatened, "You better vote for me next month or you'll be sorry!" When I asked him what he was running for, he answered, "Homeroom teacher."

October 16 9C was sent down to the basement for a fire drill. They were the only class to go, so you can guess whose idea the whole thing was. They didn't come back until the afternoon relay races. I think I know why we never got our assembly seats back, and why we still haven't been given plain old schoolwork, as I suggested. It's simple mathematics. There are 32 kids in 9C, and 31 kids in our class. We were outnumbered and outsuggested!

October 19 What a day! First, our water balloon fight was called off. Then, at eleven o'clock, people from the board of education broke down the front door and took over the school. At first they thought that our computer principal had <u>malfunctioned</u>. But, as it turns out, we were sent the wrong computer. We should have gotten the one that went out to the Midwest, and they should have gotten ours. *We* got the diplomat, and *they* got the dictator! Nobody would have discovered the mistake if our principal hadn't ordered ten tons of popcorn for the hot lunch program.

November 14 The last three weeks have been great! I love doing math, history, and English again. I feel as if the first month of school was all a bad dream. I'd better save this journal, or else no one will ever believe what happened. Of course, I can always show people the scar where Cindy's snake bit me.

November 16 Something's wrong again. I saw Miss James crying, and she wouldn't tell me why.

November 18 I found out why.

GLORIA WILLIS TEACHERS FIRED

IN A SURPRISE MOVE, THE NEW PRINCIPAL OF THE GLORIA WILLIS JUNIOR HIGH SCHOOL FIRED ALL OF THE SCHOOL'S TEACHERS. WHEN ASKED WHY THE TEACHERS WERE FIRED, T12H2679DELTA ANSWERED, " I HAD TO. ALL THEY DID FOR THE PAST MONTH WAS PLAY GAMES, WATCH MOVIES, EAT COTTON CANDY, AND CAMPAIGN FOR THEIR JOBS." WHEN ASKED IF REPLACEMENTS COULD BE FOUND QUICKLY, T12H2679DELTA ANSWERED, "WITHOUT A DOUBT! MANY OF THEIR REPLACEMENTS HAVE ALREADY BEEN DELIVERED."

RECALLING FACTS

1. What is the setting of the story?

   _____

   _____

2. Why was Gloria Willis Junior High School getting a new principal?

   _____

   _____

3. How did the new principal arrive?

   _____

   _____

4. Where, and how, is the second Delta computer being used?

   _____

   _____

5. Are the two Delta computers alike or different? Explain.

   _____

   _____

   _____

   _____

6. Draw a line to match each word with its meaning.

   coincidence   failed to work as programmed

   aerobics   events happening at about the same time that seem to be connected but really are not

   malfunctioned   physical exercises that improve the circulation of the blood

1. Why was Carmen sorry that she told Milos about the suggestion box?

   _____

2. How did life at Gloria Willis Junior High School change with the delivery
   of the new principal?

   _____

   _____

   _____

3. Identify the following statements as fact or opinion. Write *F* or *O* on the lines provided.

   _____ Luis Garcia says that once they get a bad idea in one school, they usually
   take it around to all the others.

   _____ Miss James told us there would be an election in school next month.

   _____ I think we're in big, big trouble at Gloria Willis—really gigantic trouble.

   _____ The last three weeks have been great! I love doing math, history,
   and English again.

4. **a.** How did Carmen feel about Dellie when it first arrived?

   _____

   _____

   b. How did Carmen feel about Dellie a few weeks later?

   _____

   _____

   c. How did Carmen feel when the board of education discovered that the
   wrong computer had been delivered to the school?

   _____

   _____

5. Why was Miss James fired?

   _____

   _____

   _____

6. Do you think a computer could be a good assistant to a principal? Explain.

   _____

   _____

   _____

In a story told from the first-person point of view, the reader is limited to the narrator's thoughts and feelings about an event. You may go back to the story to answer the questions below.

1. Who is the narrator of the story? _____

_____

2. Is the narrator a participant in the story's events or an outsider? Explain.

_____

_____

_____

3. Why is first-person a good point of view from which to tell this story?

_____

_____

_____

4. In the journal entries, the narrator reveals thoughts and feelings about what is going on at Gloria Willis. List two or three of the narrator's thoughts about having a computer principal.

_____

_____

_____

_____

5. Why does the reader not know how the other students felt, or what they thought, about the computer?

_____

_____

_____

_____

6. Why is it not possible for Carmen to tell in her journal entry how Miss James felt?

_____

_____

_____

▶ **Real Life Connections** Write your opinion on having the teachers in your school replaced by computers. Use the first-person point of view.

Making Generalizations

___ Reading a Social Studies Selection ___

▶ Background Information

The ideas of many scientists led to the development of today's computer. The use of computers in education, government, industry, medicine, and at home is constantly increasing.

Before reading the selection, preview it. Read the headings and study the pictures. As you read, pay attention to the facts. They are important in understanding the development of the computer. However, in order to understand fully the computer's origin and development, you will have to **make generalizations** as you read.

▶ Skill Focus

Facts are an important part of history, but facts alone cannot provide you with a complete understanding of historical developments. You must be able to draw a principle from a limited sampling of facts or ideas. A principle is a main idea statement that covers all the facts or ideas in the sampling. This principle is called a generalization. The process is called **making generalizations**.

Examine the following facts.

- Many schools use personal computers.
- Robots are used instead of people to produce some parts of automobiles.
- Banks communicate information about accounts using network computers.
- Video games are a popular form of entertainment.

The generalization below can be made based on these four facts:

> The computer is changing the way people learn, work, communicate, and play.

▶ Word Clues

Sometimes you may read selections that have a specialized vocabulary. If there are no context clues to help you understand the specialized words, there may be a glossary.

Read the sentence below.

> The Computer Revolution, well underway for some time, has brought about changes more far-reaching than those of the Industrial Revolution.

Suppose you do not know the meaning of the word *computer*. There are no context clues in the sentence to help you. You will need to turn to the glossary for help. The glossary defines the technical words in a selection. A glossary entry for *computer* tells you what a computer is.

> **computer** electronic device used to calculate, store and select data, and perform operations using stored instructions and data

If no glossary is provided, you will have to look up the words in a dictionary.

Use the **glossary** following the selection to find the meaning of the underlined words in the selection. Using the glossary is like using a special, short dictionary.

▶ Strategy Tip

Use the glossary following "From the Abacus to the Microcomputer" to help you with the specialized vocabulary in this lesson. However, you should try first to figure out the meaning of the new word by looking at the words around it.

From the Abacus to the Microcomputer

The Computer Revolution, well underway for some time, has brought about changes more far-reaching than those of the Industrial Revolution. What makes this revolution so astonishing is that the computer did not exist 60 years ago.

Many say that the computer is a modern invention. However, many of the ideas used in computer design date back several hundred years. There has always been a need for efficient and accurate counting. Originally, people used their fingers for counting. But as their needs became more complex, this method was replaced by more sophisticated devices.

Pascal's *Machine Arithmétique* (1647) was the world's first calculating machine.

Abacus

At least 2,500 years ago, the Chinese discovered that they could handle large numbers more easily by sliding little beads on strings. Their invention, the abacus, is still in use. This early mechanical <u>calculator</u> consists of a hand-held rectangular frame. In the frame are several fixed rods strung with movable beads. Numbers are recorded by moving the beads. A skilled abacus operator can easily keep pace with a person using an office calculating machine.

The abacus has been in use since ancient times.

Machine Arithmétique

In 1647, the French mathematician Blaise Pascal invented the world's first calculating machine that could add and subtract. The machine, which he called *Machine Arithmétique,* was based on gear-driven counterwheels. Its operation was similar to that of the odometer, or speedometer, in today's automobile. Similar gear-driven counterwheels were employed in mechanical calculators that were developed over the next 300 years.

Analytical Engine

Charles P. Babbage, an English mathematician born in 1792, was the first to move toward a machine that could go beyond addition and subtraction. In 1833, he tried to construct the first <u>digital</u> computer. He called this machine the Analytical Engine. It had all the features of a modern general-purpose computer, including memory, control, and <u>input/output</u> capabilities. In one minute, it could do 60 additions or subtractions. Most important of all, its operating procedures could be changed at will—the Analytical Engine was programmable!

Unfortunately, Babbage was unable to get the necessary support to continue his project. He died in 1871, frustrated and unhappy. However, his foresight won him recognition that he never lived to see.

Punched Cards and the Tabulating Machine

Development of punched cards and tabulating machines to process them was stimulated by the needs of the United States Census Bureau. In 1880, the census was taken as required every ten years by the Constitution. By 1885, the Census Bureau was still struggling to tabulate the collected facts of the 1880 census. It was soon apparent that this process would take longer than the ten-year span between censuses. A faster way of performing the task was needed.

Herman Hollerith, a statistician with the Census Bureau, devised a method of recording the census <u>data</u> on a strip of paper. His method was quite simple. Information was coded on a strip of paper by means of a series of punched holes in a planned pattern, with each hole having a specific meaning.

This coding system quickly proved to be an efficient method of recording information. The paper strips were soon replaced by three-by-five-inch cards, each containing the entire record of an individual or a family. These cards were the forerunners of punch cards and were called punched cards. To process these coded cards, Hollerith devised a tabulating machine capable of processing approximately 65 cards per minute.

The use of the punched card and tabulating machine saved so much money and time that Hollerith adapted his census tabulator to commercial work. To this end, he organized the Tabulating Machine Company, which later merged with other companies to become the International Business Machines Corporation (IBM).

The First Computers

In 1937, Harvard physicist Howard H. Aiken, with the aid of IBM, constructed a computing device. It performed arithmetic operations on data input using Hollerith punched cards. This machine, MARK I, was an early form of today's digital computer.

✔ By 1947, the University of Pennsylvania had built ENIAC (Electronic Numerical Integrator and Calculator). ENIAC filled a space as large as a two-car garage, gobbled up 140,000 watts of electricity, and had

Hollerith's punched card tabulating machine was first used for the 1880 census.

18,000 vacuum tubes. These tubes were large and costly and produced a lot of heat. While ENIAC worked 1,000 times faster than MARK I, it had one major weakness. To perform different operations, it had to be manually rewired—a task that could take several days.

Hungarian-born John Von Neumann suggested feeding data into the computer through a keyboard. The first commercial computer to have this input device was UNIVAC I (Universal Automatic Computer). In 1951, UNIVAC I became the first mass-produced, commercially available computer.

✗ The most important contributions to the development of computers were made by John Von Neumann. His work resulted in improvements in areas from the computer's design to its electronic circuitry. With others, he developed the ideas of the <u>stored program</u> and the <u>binary</u> number system. These concepts are used in the most modern computers.

Modern Computer Generations

In recent years, computer developments have been far-reaching and numerous. Because of this rapid progress, computers have been categorized by generations, each generation featuring a significant advance over the previous generation.

First Generation (1942–1959) These computers used vacuum tubes for the storage of data. The vacuum tube was bulky, caused tremendous overheating problems, and was unreliable. These "maxi" or <u>mainframe computers</u> were large and expensive.

Second Generation (1959–1965) These computers replaced the vacuum tube with the transistor. A transistor is an electronic device made up of semiconducting materials, mostly crystals of germanium or silicon, that control the flow of electric currents. Second-generation computers were small and worked fast. They could perform a single operation in one-tenth the time it took computers that used vacuum tubes. With the second generation of computers, manufacturers began producing business-oriented computers with more efficient storage and faster input/output capabilities. These minicomputers were smaller, more reliable, and less costly than earlier models.

Computers have advanced quickly from the large mainframe computers that took up entire rooms to small desk-sized and laptop computers to multi-media systems.

Third Generation (1965–1970) These computers had microminiaturized integrated circuits on a chip, or plate, as small as a dime and as thin as paper. The components on the chip were so small that they were hardly visible to the naked eye. In addition, new input/output devices were able to communicate with computers over great distances via telephone lines, display pictures on a televisionlike screen, and accept voice input and respond in the same manner. These <u>microcomputers</u> also had tremendous memory capacities. They could work so fast that their operation was measured in <u>nanoseconds</u>.

Fourth Generation (1970–present) These computers brought the <u>microprocessor</u> into use. Essential to the microprocessor is the chip that contains the integrated circuits and the whole <u>central processing unit</u> (CPU) of a simple computer.

The Future Is Now

Microelectronics has moved from the 1940s garage-size computers to the 1990s portable and home computers, complete with <u>CD-ROM</u> drives and <u>modems</u>. People with no technical background can use computers to do a variety of tasks—from performing complex calculations to tracking a personal budget. The home computer can be linked to the <u>Internet</u>, and a fellow computer user anywhere is only a click or a keystroke away. Soon communication by computer will be as common as conversations over the telephone.

Glossary

binary having a two-number system consisting of digits 0 and 1

calculator machine that rapidly adds, subtracts, multiplies, and divides, often by electronic means

CD-ROM (Compact Disc-Read Only Memory) an optical disk containing text and multimedia data that can be retrieved by a laser beam

central processing unit control center for an entire computer system

computer electronic device used to calculate, store, and select data

data information or instructions that a computer can interpret

digital having data in number form

input data inserted or fed into a computer

Internet a worldwide computer network of networks with millions of subscribers

mainframe computer largest and most powerful of the early computers

microprocessor a chip having the capabilities of a simple computer

modem a device for sending data, usually over telephone lines, between computers

nanosecond one-billionth of a second

output information that has been processed through a computer

stored program series of commands that directs what the computer does

---

RECALLING FACTS

1. Sequence the following events in the order in which they occurred.

   _____ construction of Babbage's Analytical Engine

   _____ invention of the abacus

   _____ creation of ENIAC

   _____ invention of Pascal's *Machine Arithmétique*

   _____ production of UNIVAC I

   _____ development of Hollerith's punched cards

2. How have the stages in the development of computer technology been labeled?

   _____

   _____

3. Reread the paragraph marked with an X. Underline its main idea. Then circle two details that support the main idea.

4. How were first-generation computers different from the second-generation?

   _____

   _____

5. Write three sentences, each using one or more of the specialized vocabulary words listed below.

   calculator   computer   binary

   data   digital   nanosecond

   a. _____

   _____

   b. _____

   _____

   c. _____

   _____

INTERPRETING FACTS

1. The ancient Chinese had a need for efficient and accurate counting. Their need resulted in the invention of the abacus. Compare their need with present-day needs.

   _____

   _____

2. Reread the paragraph with a check mark next to it. Then circle the letter of the statement that best states the main idea of the paragraph.

   a. ENIAC worked faster than the earlier MARK I.

   b. The first fully electronic digital computer worked much faster than earlier types but was large and difficult to program.

   c. The early electronic computers contained thousands of vacuum tubes.

SKILL FOCUS

Following the box below are three groups of facts. Read each group of facts carefully. Then from the generalizations listed in the box, choose the statement that is the most appropriate generalization for each group and write the letter of the statement on the line provided. You may go back to the selection if necessary.

---

a. Computers have become smaller, more efficient, and more available.

b. The computer's influence is evident in business, medicine, and education.

c. The limitless potential of the computer will continue to change our future.

d. A standard memory chip can store about 300 pages of text.

e. Many features of today's computers are the result of discoveries made many years ago.

---

1. **Facts** Computers are used to store employee payroll data, such as weekly salary, taxes, and benefits contributions.
   Computers are used to diagnose medical problems and to monitor patients' progress.
   Computer-assisted instruction is found in some elementary and secondary schools.

   Generalization _____

2. **Facts** The abacus was the first mechanical calculator.
   Babbage's Analytical Engine was programmable.
   Hollerith's punched cards and tabulating machine were used to compile information for the 1880 census.

   Generalization _____

3. **Facts** Transistors reduced the size of the computer and increased its working speed.
   Integrated circuitry and the microchip made communication possible over great distances via telephone lines.
   The microprocessor led to the development of portable and home computers.

   Generalization _____

4. **Facts** The typewriter is being replaced by the word processor.
   Information once found in books and libraries is being stored on tapes and disks.
   Two-way teleconference screens eliminate the need for traveling to meetings.
   Telecommunications provide the homebound with the means of earning a livelihood.

   Generalization _____

▶ Real Life Connections How can using a computer help you learn?

Inferences

___ Reading a Science Selection ___

▶ Background Information

As you read the following selection about computers, pay close attention to the facts. Use the facts to infer information that is not directly stated in the selection.

▶ Skill Focus

Sometimes you can **infer**, or figure out, information that is not stated directly in a selection. Read the following paragraphs. Try to infer what the term *computer age* means.

John was feeling sorry for himself. Two of his best friends had just gotten computer games. John really wanted one, but his parents wouldn't agree to buy it.

"I keep hearing that this is the <u>computer age</u>," said John. "If it is, I'm sure not living in it."

"You're surrounded by computers," said his mother. John looked surprised. "What do you mean?"

"Think about it," replied his mother. "You have a digital clock radio. What controls it? Think about the heater in our car. Remember

what the salesclerk said about it? And what about the thermostat on our furnace? What controls that? You are more a part of the computer age than you think."

The following clues can help you infer the meaning of the term *computer age*. John's best friends have computer games. John does not. John believes his friends are part of the computer age while he is not. You can infer that *computer age* means "a time when many people have and use computers."

You could infer other things from these paragraphs. You could infer that many common things are controlled by computers. The following clue could help you figure this out: John's mother hinted that computers were part of their digital clock radio, car, and furnace.

In your reading, you will find it easier to infer information if you go through the following steps.

1. Read carefully.
2. Think about what you've read. Be sure you understand the information that is stated.

3. Read again and look for clues to information not stated.
4. Put together information stated with information that you already know. Use clues to help you make inferences.

▶ Word Clues

Sometimes special terms are explained in a paragraph and also shown in a diagram. When this happens, study both the text and the diagram to help you understand the special terms.

Use **diagram** clues as well as **context** clues to find out the meaning of the three underlined terms in Figure 1 on page 166.

▶ Strategy Tip

Before you read "What is a Computer?" preview the boldfaced words and the labels in the diagrams. These words are an important part of computer language. Knowing such words will help you live in "the computer age!"

WHAT IS A COMPUTER?

1. A computer is an electronic machine that can store and handle information and solve problems. You could think of a computer as a file cabinet, information organizer, and problem-solver all rolled into one.

2. Computers are sometimes called electronic brains because of the kinds of work they do. A computer can do many of the things that the human brain can do. However, a computer cannot truly understand ideas. It cannot create, or make things up. Unlike human beings, a computer has no imagination. The information that goes into a computer comes from people or from machines controlled by people. The problems computers work out also come from people. Even the methods for working out the problems come from people. Computers can do only what people have built them to do.

The first computers could only compute, or mathematically work out, number problems.

3. A computer has certain advantages over the human brain. In some ways, a computer is much faster and more efficient than the human brain. The fastest computers can solve millions of problems in a few seconds. Also, computers do not make many mistakes. They can handle one dull problem after another without getting tired or bored. They are not distracted by noise or other interruptions.

4. The first computers could do only one kind of job. They could **compute**, or mathematically work out, number problems. Today's computers can do much, much more. They can store company records and make out company payrolls. They can be used as teaching aids. They can help pilots fly. They can help weather forecasters predict weather. They can ring up a bill at the supermarket. They can help the grocer keep track of stock. They can deal with words as well as numbers. If a number or word problem can be worked out in a series of fixed steps, a computer can do it.

Types of Computers

5. Not all computers are the same. They don't all work in the same way. They aren't all used for the same purposes.

Digital Computers

6. The most common computers are **digital** computers. The word *digital* comes from the word *digit*, which means "number." Before information goes into the computer, it is changed into a code in which groups of digits stand for letters, symbols, and numbers. The coded information goes into the machine as electronic signals. The computer works by reading, or counting, these signals. Most digital computers are general-purpose machines. They can do many kinds of work. For instance, a computer might store information about the people in a company. It might also process paychecks.

Analog Computers

7. **Analog** computers work by measuring physical happenings. They might measure the flow of gas and air in an engine. They might measure the speed and direction of an airplane. They change these measurements into electronic signals for the computer to process. Most analog computers are special-purpose machines. They are built to do one kind of job.

Hybrid Computers

8. Some computers both measure and count. These computers are called **hybrid** computers.

Components of Computers

9. Each digital computer has three basic components, or parts. The basic components are made up of many complex parts. These basic mechanical parts of a computer are called its **hardware**.

Central Processing Unit (CPU)

10. The main component of any computer is its **central processing unit**, or **CPU**. It is in the CPU that information and instructions are stored and processed. The CPU has a memory, or storage, unit. This unit stores information and instructions. It holds information and instructions until they are

Figure 1. The three basic components of a digital computer are the CPU, the input equipment, and the output equipment.

needed. In some computers, the memory is a group of magnetic cores, or doughnut-shaped rings. In others, it is a magnetic tape, disk, or drum. Information appears on tapes and disks as magnetic spots. In the smallest computers, the memory, or even the whole CPU, may be on a tiny piece of equipment called a **chip**.

11. The CPU also has an arithmetic, or logic, unit. This is the working part of the computer. It sorts information and computes —adds, subtracts, and so on.

12. The control unit of the CPU controls the work of the computer. It is the "captain" of the computer. It gets instructions from the memory. Then it tells the memory what information to send to the arithmetic unit. Finally, it tells the arithmetic unit how to process the information.

Input Equipment

13. **Input** means information that is fed into a computer. Before a computer can do any work, information and instructions must go into it. Such information and instruction for a computer is called **software**. The input equipment takes information and instruction from the outside world. Then it puts it into code for the computer to use. Special keyboards serve as input equipment on most home computers.

Output Equipment

14. **Output** means information delivered from a computer according to coded instruction. Information can come out of a computer in many forms. It can show up on a

display screen, or it can be turned out on paper by a printer.

15. Often input and output equipment is attached to the CPU. However, input and output equipment can also be far away from the CPU. Then they are connected by cables, wires, or remote-control equipment. Remote-control is the ability to control the operation of a machine by means of radio waves.

16. The mechanical components of a computer are called hardware. The instructions and information that go into or come out of a computer are called software.

Computer Codes

17. Information and instructions enter the computer in the form of electronic signals. The computer knows only two signals. In many, these are *on* and *off*. Therefore, all information going into the machine must be put into an "on/off" code.

18. In one computer code, the digit *0* stands for *off*; the digit *1* stands for *on*. Each letter, symbol, and number that goes into the computer has its own code of eight *0*s and *1*s. Figure 2 shows that 00000010 is the code for the number *2*. This passes into the computer as *off, off, off, off, off, off, on, off*. All the *on*s show up in the memory as magnetic spots. All the *off*s show up as blank spaces.

19. Each digit in the computer code is called a **bit**. A group of eight bits is called a **byte**. You can tell if a computer has a large or small memory by the number of bytes it can hold. A kilobyte is 1000 bytes. A typical personal computer might have anywhere from 1 to 16 megabytes. A megabyte is 1 million bytes.

1 = 00000001	A = 01000001
2 = 00000010	B = 01000010
3 = 00000011	C = 01000011
4 = 00000100	(–) = 00101101
5 = 00000101	(+) = 00101011

Figure 2. These are some examples of an eight-bit computer code. Each number, letter, or symbol has a code of eight digits.

1. What is a computer?

   _____

   _____

   _____

2. What are the three main components of a computer?

   _____

   _____

   _____

3. What is hardware? software?

   _____

   _____

   _____

4. What does each component do?

   _____

   _____

   _____

5. Circle the letter next to each of the following that a computer can do.
   a. think   c. create
   b. solve problems   d. understand

6. What is a byte?

   _____

   _____

7. Name three kinds of computers.

   _____

   _____

8. Draw a line to match each term with its explanation.

   output equipment   computer component that sorts information and solves problems

   input equipment   computer component that delivers information

   arithmetic unit   computer component that receives information and instructions

INTERPRETING FACTS

1. What kind of computer would be used to keep track of air temperature and humidity?

   _____

   _____

Circle the letter next to the correct answer.

2. In the future, computers will probably be
   a. larger and able to do more.
   b. the same size and able to do less.
   c. smaller and able to do more.

3. In the future, computers will probably replace people who
   a. do large projects keeping track of things.
   b. solve problems that require inventing mathematical theories.
   c. create new ideas for designing things.

Decide which statements can be inferred from the numbered paragraph or paragraphs listed below. Put a check mark next to the statement or statements. On the lines that follow, write the phrase or sentence from the paragraph or paragraphs that helped you decide. Then explain how you inferred the information.

Paragraph 2 (check two)

a. _____ A computer cannot store as much information as the human brain.

b. _____ A computer is like the human brain in some ways but not in others.

c. _____ The human brain can think, understand, create, and process information.

Clue _____

_____

Explanation _____

_____

_____

Paragraph 3 (check two)

a. _____ Some human beings have difficulty keeping facts in their heads.

b. _____ Human beings get tired and bored from handling dull problems.

c. _____ Human beings sometimes make mistakes when they handle dull problems.

Clue _____

_____

Explanation _____

_____

_____

Paragraphs 17 and 18 (check one)

a. _____ Computer codes are all the same.

b. _____ Computer codes can be read by anyone.

c. _____ Computer codes stand for different things depending on the spacing of the *off*s.

Clue _____

_____

_____

Explanation _____

_____

▶ Real Life Connections Make a prediction: What size computer will you use ten years from today?

Computer Language

Reading a Mathematics Selection

▶ Background Information

In the 1960s, the National Aeronautics Space Administration, or NASA, used computers during their many space flights. These computers helped make landing on the moon a reality. However, these computers were bulky and expensive. As a matter of fact, they took up entire rooms.

Today there are **laptop** computers (computers designed to fit on a person's lap) that have the same capabilities as a room full of computers and are relatively inexpensive.

How is all this possible? The keyboard of a computer looks like the keyboard of a typewriter. However, the similarities stop there. A computer can do much more than a typewriter. It can make calculations in a matter of seconds that would take a person hours, or even days, to complete.

Computers are programmed to do many different things. This is done by typing in certain phrases. These phrases tell the computer what to do. A computer language is a group of these phrases. In

"Understanding Computer Language," you will learn about the computer language called **BASIC**.

▶ Skill Focus

In order for a computer to perform, it must be programmed, or instructed, through its input devices. In other words, you "talk" to a computer using its input devices. This talking is done in a special language that the computer understands. By giving instructions in a computer language, you could ask a computer to solve a problem. The computer would present the solution to the problem through its output devices.

There are many types of computers. Programmers are people who "talk" with computers in different languages. Although different languages are used to program computers, all computers process information the same way. Computers use binary numbers. The word *binary* means "a number system that has 2 as its base." This number system uses only two digits, 0 and 1. The binary number system is used as the basis for computing

because the digits 0 and 1 can be represented by electric current that is either turned on (1) or turned off (0).

▶ Word Clues

When reading "Understanding Computer Language," look for these important words: *input devices, output devices, central processing unit, BASIC, PRINT, LET, END, RUN, GOTO,* and *compiler.* They will help you to understand more about computers.

▶ Strategy Tip

As you read the selection, keep in mind that learning a computer language is something like learning a foreign language. The words may be familiar to you, but you need to learn their meanings as they apply to computers.

Understanding Computer Language

Computers are used because they can solve problems more quickly than people can. A computer gets its instructions from various **input devices,** such as a **keyboard,** a **mouse,** a **light scanner,** and a **light pen.** The instructions present a problem to the computer. The computer presents the solution on a monitor. The solution can also be delivered by a printer or a modem. These viewing mechanisms are called output devices. The instructions are carried out in the **central processing unit,** or **CPU.**

A programmer needs to be able to communicate with the computer in a language that it understands. Some computer languages, such as COBOL, FORTRAN, C, and C++, are used for business. Others, such as LISP and PROLOG, are used in artificial intelligence. BASIC (Beginners All-purpose Symbolic Instruction Code), is the simplest to learn and easiest to use.

Learning BASIC is like learning a foreign language. Commands in BASIC have very precise meanings. The computer understands commands only if they are written in a certain way.

Each line of a program has a number. The lines are read by the computer in the order in which they are numbered. After the program has been put in, the programmer types *RUN.* Then the program is interpreted by the CPU, and the output is shown.

For example, *PRINT* tells the computer to write whatever follows. The programmer might input this statement.

10 PRINT "I AM A COMPUTER"

The output would be I AM A COMPUTER.

The programmer might input these lines.
10 LET X = 32
20 PRINT X
30 END

The output would be 32.

Line 10 puts the number 32 into the memory of the computer. The memory labels that number as X. Line 20 tells the computer to output whatever is in memory X.

The last line of a program is always *END.* It tells the CPU that the program is over.

The programmer could input this program.
10 PRINT "I AM A"
20 PRINT "COMPUTER"
30 GOTO 20
40 END

The command *GOTO* tells the computer to go back to line 20. The computer would read line 10, line 20, and line 30 and then go back to line 20, on to line 30, back to line 20, on to line 30, and so on. This is called a **loop** because the computer makes a circle as it reads the lines. The program would never end unless the programmer stopped it by pressing a key on the keyboard. The output would look like this:

I AM A
COMPUTER
COMPUTER
COMPUTER (and so on)

When a program is put into the computer, the instructions are translated into a language that the machine understands. This is called a machine language. The **compiler** translates the numbers and letters of machine language into **binary numbers.** *Zero* can be represented as a broken circuit—an electric current that is turned off. *One* can be represented as a completed circuit—an electric current that is turned on. All the numbers and letters of a language can be changed into current turned off and current turned on.

RECALLING FACTS

1. Name three input devices. _____

2. Explain the following commands.

   a. PRINT _____

   b. END _____

   c. GOTO _____

1. What do the quotation marks do in this line? 10 PRINT "HOW ARE YOU?"

_____

_____

2. What would the computer print if you gave the command PRINT X? PRINT "X"?

_____

_____

SKILL FOCUS

A. Write the letter of the output on the line next to the input.

Input	Output
_____ **1.** 10 PRINT "HELLO" 20 PRINT "GOODBYE" 30 END	**a.** HELLO 5 GOODBYE
_____ **2.** 10 LET X = 7 20 LET Y = 2 30 PRINT X + Y 40 END	**b.** X + Y = 9
_____ **3.** 10 LET X = 7 20 LET Y = 2 30 PRINT "X + Y =" 40 PRINT X + Y 50 END	**c.** 9
_____ **4.** 10 LET X = 9 20 PRINT "THE ANSWER IS"; X 30 END	**d.** HELLO GOODBYE
_____ **5.** 10 PRINT "HELLO" 20 LET X = 5 30 PRINT X 40 PRINT "GOODBYE" 50 END	**e.** THE ANSWER IS 9

B. Complete the following programs so that they will have the output shown.

1. Output: A COMPUTER MAKES YOUR LIFE EASIER.

Program: 10 PRINT _____

_____

20 _____

2. Output: I AM
YOUR
FRIEND

Program: 10 PRINT _____

20 PRINT _____

30 PRINT _____

40 _____

3. Output: HELLO
GOODBYE
HELLO
GOODBYE
(and so on)

Program: 10 PRINT _____

20 PRINT _____

30 GOTO _____

40 _____

▶ **Real Life Connections** What computer languages are used on the computers in your school or local library?

Reference Books

You use **reference books** to find all kinds of information about a subject that you are studying or want to know more about. You need to know the kind of information contained in each reference book so that you can select the one you need. By using the right reference books, you can locate the kind of information you need.

Suppose that some friends of yours are discussing a gibbon and you don't know what a gibbon is. You can find the word *gibbon* in the **dictionary**. You already know that a dictionary defines words. It also shows how words are spelled, pronounced, and divided into syllables, and what parts of speech they are. Because many people do not know what a gibbon looks like, some dictionaries include an illustration with the entry.

Gibbon is the smallest of the apes. It also ranges over a wider area than the other members of the ape family— the chimpanzee, gorilla, and orangutan. The gibbon lives in the forests of the Indian state of Assam, and in Burma, Thailand, Malaysia, Indonesia, and elsewhere in Southeast Asia. There are several species of gibbons. All have long arms and legs, but no tail. A gibbon weighs about 15 pounds (7 kilograms) and stands about 3 feet (91 centimeters) high. It ranges from black to pale brown.

Gibbons live in the tops of trees and rarely come to the ground. They eat fruits and leaves. Gibbons use their arms to swing from branch to branch. They also walk on top of tree branches using only their legs. This way of walking is similar to that of human beings. Gibbons live in family groups that usually consist of a male, a female, and one or two of their young. A gibbon family claims an area called a *territory* and uses loud calls and songs to warn other families to stay away.

From the *World Book Encyclopedia.* © 1996 World Book, Inc. By permission of the publisher.

gib•bon (gib′ ən) *n.* a small ape of southeastern Asia, with very long arms.

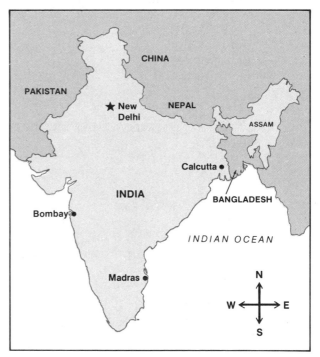

After you learn what the word *gibbon* means, you may want to find out more about the animal. You may become curious about how small an ape it is, exactly what part of southeastern Asia it is from, or if it can be found at a zoo. The next reference book that you would use is an **encyclopedia** because it contains articles on many different subjects. An encyclopedia would provide an explanation of a gibbon that is more detailed than a dictionary definition.

After you have read the encyclopedia article for *gibbon,* you may become curious

about Assam, one of the places where the gibbon lives. You may want to look at a map to see the location of Assam in India. The best reference book to check is an atlas. An **atlas** contains different kinds of maps.

Once you learn where Assam is, you may want some specific information about India and its size and population. To locate this kind of information, you would use an almanac. An **almanac** is a book with the most up-to-date information on many different subjects. Although an encyclopedia may provide some of the same information, it may not be as current. The information in an **almanac** is more current than information found in other references because it is published every year. An almanac contains weather reports, statistics, and facts about the United States and other countries, current events, sports facts, world records, and other interesting information.

Area and Population by Country
Mid-1993 Estimates

Country	Area[1]	Population	Country	Area[1]	Population
Afghanistan	250,000	17,400,000	Hungary	35,920	10,300,000
Albania	11,100	3,300,000	Iceland	39,770	300,000
Algeria	919,590	27,300,000	India	1,269,340	897,400,000
Angola	481,350	9,500,000	Indonesia	741,100	187,600,000
Antigua and Barbuda	170	100,000	Iran	636,290	62,800,000
Argentina	1,068,300	33,500,000	Iraq	167,920	19,200,000

Complete each sentence by underlining the name of the correct reference book. More than one answer may be correct.

1. If you want to know how to spell the word *cantaloupe,* you should use the _____ .

   atlas   dictionary   almanac

2. If you want to find out what kinds of crops are grown in South America,

   you should use the _____ or the _____ .

   almanac   atlas   encyclopedia

3. If you want to know how many people were married in the United States

   in 1982, you should use the _____ .

   atlas   encyclopedia   almanac

4. If you want to find out how to pronounce the word *kayak,* you should use the _____ .

   encyclopedia   almanac   dictionary

5. If you want to learn which types of birds live in cold climates, you should use the _____ .

   dictionary   encyclopedia   almanac

6. If you want to find out how many miles (kilometers) it is from Quincy,

   Massachusetts, to Newport, Rhode Island, you should use the _____ .

   atlas   dictionary   encyclopedia

7. If you want to know what kind of boat a schooner is, you should

   use the _____ or the _____ .

   encyclopedia   almanac   dictionary

8. If you want to see how to divide the word *molecule* into syllables, use the _____ .

   atlas   dictionary   almanac

9. If you want to compare the population of Iceland in 1970 to that of last year, you should
   use the _____ .

   dictionary   almanac   atlas

Reading a Job Application

When you apply for a job, many companies will require you to fill out a job application. A **job application** is a written form that asks for information about your work experience, your education, and your interests.

Study the sample job application below.

C AL COMPUTER OMPANY	APPLICATION FOR EMPLOYMENT			(Type or print in ink)

PERSONAL

Name	Last LORENZ	First DALE	Middle/Maiden SARAH	Telephone 555-7431
Address	Number 1154 / Street 23rd Street	City SANTA MONICA,	State CA / Zip 90404	Social Security No. 219-68-8429

EDUCATION

	Name and Location	Dates Attended From / To	Diploma Received
High School	SCOTTSDALE HIGH SCHOOL SCOTTSDALE, AZ	9/85 6/88	HIGH SCHOOL DIPLOMA
College	ROLLINS COLLEGE SCOTTSDALE, AZ	9/88 6/92	B.S.
Other	COMPUTER TRAINING INSTITUTE SANTA MONICA, CA	9/94 1/95	COMPUTER CERTIFICATE

Hobbies and Interest   SWIMMING, PLAYING THE PIANO, SPEAKING SPANISH

EMPLOYMENT RECORD (Start with last job)

Name and Location of Employer	Dates From / To	Job Title	Name of Supervisor
LINDSEY AND STERLING ACCOUNTANTS SANTA MONICA, CA	1/95 7/95	BOOKKEEPER	BERT GOLDBERG
DAILY NEWS SCOTTSDALE, AZ	7/92 8/94	WORD PROCESSOR	ROSA ALVAREZ

REFERENCES (Not former employers)

	Name	Address	Telephone
1.	MS. DIANE BARTON	90 WILSHIRE BLVD. LOS ANGELES, CA	555-4418
2.	DR. LOUIS GRAYSON	880 W. CAMELBACK SCOTTSDALE, AZ	602-555-3099

EMPLOYMENT DESIRED

Position COMPUTER PROGRAMMER   Date you can start 8/17/95   (Check one) Full-time ✔ Part-time _____

Today's Date 8/10/95   Signature Dale S. Lorenz

Most job applications begin with a section for personal information. The first space is for your first, middle, and last names. Sometimes a married woman writes her maiden name, or her last name before she was married, in the space for the middle name. Spaces are provided for your address and telephone number and your social security number. Everyone needs a social security number to get a job.

Most job applications have sections to fill out about your education or training. Certain jobs require a particular type of education or training.

Job applications also have a section on the jobs that you have held in the past. This section may be labeled "Work Experience" or "Employment Record."

Applications often require you to provide references. References are people who know you well enough to give information about you and how you might perform on a job. Family members and friends should not be listed as references. Possible references might include a teacher; a family doctor; or a pastor, priest, or rabbi. You should ask these people if you can use them as references before you do so.

Applications may ask for other information, such as your interests and hobbies—for example, playing tennis or speaking French.

A section labeled "Employment Desired" may provide a space for the name of the job that you want and the date that you can begin. You usually sign your name at the end of the application.

Print in ink or type your answers on the application. A neat application with complete answers will make a good impression on an employer.

Correct grammar and spelling and clear expression will also make a good impression.

A. Circle the letter next to the phrase that correctly completes each sentence.

1. The debating club, the swim team, and cheerleading are examples of
   a. extracurricular activities.   b. references.   c. hobbies.

2. An employer is a
   a. person hired by another person or company.
   b. person or company that hires people.
   c. person who can give information about your education.

3. A supervisor is a
   a. person who oversees your work.
   b. place where you have a job.
   c. family member who can give information about you.

4. An example of a good reference to use on a job application might be
   a. an employer you did not get along with.
   b. your best friend.
   c. your English teacher.

5. An application may ask for the name of your supervisor at a previous job so that this person
   a. will be informed if you get another job.
   b. may be offered the job that you applied for.
   c. may be called to confirm information about you.

6. This application does not ask for the applicant's
   a. address.   b. date of birth.   c. phone number.

7. After the applicant graduated from college, she
   a. went to the Computer Training Institute.
   b. worked for Lindscy and Sterling as a keypunch operator.
   c. worked for the *Daily News* as a word processor.

8. You can tell that the applicant does not have a job now because
   a. the ending date of her last job is before the date of the application.
   b. she said she could not start working until she left her current job.
   c. she had time to apply for another job.

B. Use the information on the application to answer each question.

1. Who filled out the application? _____

2. What job is she applying for? _____

3. What was her last job? _____

4. How long did she work at her last job? _____

5. In what place did she probably live for many years? _____
   How do you know? _____
   _____

6. How soon can she begin a new job? _____

7. According to this application, who is the employer? _____

Context Clue Words

The following words are treated as context clue words in the lessons indicated. Lessons that provide instruction in a particular context clue type include an activity requiring students to use context clues to derive word meanings. Context clue words appear in the literature, social studies, and science selections and are underlined or footnoted for ease of location.

Word	Lesson						
adept	11	Crete	1	input equipment	50	pentathlon	42
advocated	35	cultivation	22	internal	13	priority	41
aerobics	48	data	49	Internet	49	proportion	11
Apollo	1	decathlon	42	involuntary	13	public opinion	21
arithmetic unit	50	demonstrations	12	labyrinth	1	reconstruct	12
aspired	20	detention camps	21	mainframe computers	49	reflects	3
avalanche	34	digital	49	malfunctioned	48	reparations	12
blockaded	12	dismantling	12	man-of-war	21	resistance arm	43
butterfly	41	donned	2	marine	22	revive	42
calculator	49	dubious	35	microcomputers	49	revolve	3
catastrophe	33	ebbing	20	microprocessor	49	rifts	35
CD-ROM	49	effort arm	43	modems	49	rotates	3
central processing unit	49	eke	34	moderate	34	serene	11
chlorine	41	endeavor	2	moored	22	sheer	33
clamber	41	fatigue	41	moors	33	Sicily	1
coincidence	48	fulcrum	43	nanoseconds	49	spectator	2
comet	3	gradually	35	orbit	3	technicians	48
computer	49	grappling	33	origin	42	tenders	21
coordinates	13	hemispheres	13	output	49	upheaval	34
cove	20	innovations	22	output equipment	50	vastness	2
		input	49	outspoken	11	winch	20

Concept Words

In lessons that feature social studies, science, or mathematics selections, words that are unique to the content and whose meanings are essential to the selection are treated as concept words. Many of these words appear in boldface type and are often followed by a phonetic respelling and a definition.

Word	Lesson						
all together	23	compiler	51	lever	43	parasympathetic system	13
analog	50	compute	50	light pen	51	per	23
aquaculture	22	connecting nerves	13	light scanner	51	percent	36
asteroid belt	3	continental drift	35	line	4	peripheral nervous system	13
asteroids	3	data	44	lithosphere	35	perpendicular	4
asthenosphere	35	decimal	36	loop	51	plane	4
autonomic nervous system	13	dendrites	13	machine	43	planets	3
		digital	50	Mars	3	plankton	22
average	23	divided	23	mechanical advantage	43	plate tectonics	35
axon	13	Earth	3	medulla	13	Pluto	3
Barringer Meteorite	3	effort	43	Mercury	3	point	4
BASIC	51	effort distance	43	meteor	3	pulley	43
binary numbers	51	fixed pulley	43	meteorite	3	reflex action	13
bit	50	fraction	36	meteoroids	3	resistance	43
byte	50	Halley's Comet	3	mil	14	resistance distance	43
central nervous system	13	hardware	50	motor nerves	13	Saturn	3
		hybrid	50	mouse	51	sectors	44
central processing unit	50	inner planets	3	movable pulley	43	sensory nerves	13
cerebellum	13	input	50	Neptune	3	software	50
cerebrum	13	input devices	51	neuron	13	sympathetic system	13
change	36	intersect	4	ocean-floor spreading	35	theory	35
chip	50	Jupiter	3	outer planets	3	twice as much	23
circle graphs	44	keyboard	51	output	50	Uranus	3
coma	3	krill	22			Venus	3
comets	3	label	44	Pangaea	35		
		larvae	22	parallel	4		